D1490785

STRIKE FROM THE SKY

ISRAELI AIRBORNE TROOPS

VILLARD MILITARY SERIES

STRIKE FROM THE SKY

ISRAELI AIRBORNE TROOPS

Series Editor: Ashley Brown

Consultant Editors:

Brigadier-General
James L Collins Jr (Retd)

Dr John Pimlott

Brigadier-General
Edwin H Simmons USMC (Retd)

VILLARD BOOKS NEW YORK
1986

Copyright © 1986 by Orbis Publishing, London

All rights reserved under International and Pan-
American Copyright Conventions, Published in
the United States by Villard Books, a division of
Random House, Inc., New York, and
simultaneously in Canada by Random House of
Canada Limited, Toronto.

First published in Great Britain by Orbis
Publishing Limited, London

Contributing Authors

Ashley Brown
Ronnie Daniel
Rafael Eitan
Tony Gadot
Ian Westwell
Major Louis Williams

Acknowledgments

Photographs were supplied by:
Shlomo Arad, Associated Press, Balmahane,
Micha Bar-Am, Camera Press, *Daily Telegraph*
Colour Library, Deutsche Presse Agentur
Bilderdienst, Dr Jossi Faktor, Christopher Foss,
Gamma, Hanoch Guthmann, John Hillelson
Agency, Ian Hogg, Robert Hunt Library, Imperial
War Museum, Israel Government Press Office,
Israeli Defence Forces Archives, Israeli Defence
Forces Spokesman, Magnum, Photosource,
Popperfoto, Rex Features, David Rubinger, Frank
Spooner Pictures, Times Newspapers Ltd, John
Topham Picture Library, UPI/Bettmann.

The publishers would like to thank the *IDF Journal*
for permission to reproduce chapter 6, 'Raid on
Entebbe', by Major Louis Williams. A fuller
version of Major Williams' account appears in the
May 1985 issue of the *Journal*.

Front cover photograph: Israeli paratroopers, Gaza 1967
Back cover photograph: Israeli paratroopers, Golan Heights 1967
Title spread: Israeli paratrooper, Lebanon 1982

Library of Congress Catalog Card Number: 85-40985
ISBN: 0-394-74404-7

Printed in Italy
9 8 7 6 5 4 3 2
First Edition

CONTENTS

INTRODUCTION
The History of Israeli
Airborne Forces

THE ISRAELI Parachute Corps has a good claim to being considered the most successful of all modern elite units – its achievements are quite awe-inspiring. Starting with successful small-scale cross-border raids during the 1950s, the paras proved their airborne qualities with a daring drop onto the Mitla Pass in Sinai during the 1956 War. Then, in the next major confrontation between Israel and its Arab neighbours, the Six-Day War of 1967, they not only led the assault on Sinai, but also captured the Old City of Jerusalem – perhaps the most important symbol to Jews everywhere of the long history of their religion. In the 'War of Attrition' that followed the Six-Day War, Israeli paras undertook further decisive actions: raiding the PLO headquarters in Jordan in 1968, capturing a Soviet-supplied radar installation from the

Below: A platoon of Israeli paratroopers advances across desert terrain during an exercise. Israeli Defence Force reservists normally spend 40 days a year on refresher training courses.

Egyptians in 1969, and, in 1972, rescuing hostages from a hijacked aircraft on the runway at Lod Airport.

The year 1973 saw more full-scale fighting for the paras, when the combined Egyptian and Syrian attack smashed into Israel's border defences during the religious holiday of Yom Kippur. Paras spearheaded the crossing to the West Bank of the Canal that undermined the Egyptian offensive, and on the Golan front they took part in the assault on Mount Hermon, a crucial strongpoint that had been taken in the initial Syrian attacks.

The paras' actions in the Yom Kippur War had often demanded the greatest self-sacrifice. Their next major achievement, however, was one that cost a minimum of casualties – and gained the respect of the world. This was the famous Entebbe raid, Operation Thunderball (July 1976), in which a plane-load of hostages was rescued from Uganda in a sudden airborne strike that caught the hijackers completely unprepared. All but one of the hostages were rescued for the loss of only one Israeli para – the commander of the troops who successfully stormed the airport building.

The Israeli Parachute Corps, whose badge is shown above, was created by Major Yoel Palgi during the 1948 War of Independence.

He faced an enormous task: nowhere in Palestine was there a usable parachute and the Israeli Air Force had only one aircraft suitable for dropping paratroopers.

Palgi, however, was able to overcome these initial problems and was able to establish a training base at Ramat David. His call for volunteers was answered by over 100 men, most of whom had never seen a parachute. This inexperience resulted in a series of accidents and several senior officers began to doubt the wisdom of setting up a parachute unit. In the wake of this bad start, Palgi resigned. The IDF general headquarters decided to persevere with the unit and placed Yehuda Harari in command. He tightened discipline and introduced a tough 36-day training course. Under his watchful eye the paratroops became a well-schooled force, although still untested by combat. This state of affairs continued until 1954 when, shortly after their amalgamation with Unit 101 – an elite commando force – they attacked Egyptian troops at Kissufim.

Above: During World War II the British Army formed a Jewish Brigade from the Jews of Palestine. They served on the Italian front in 1945, but saw little fighting. The experience of military practices gained in this unit, however, would prove valuable in the creation of the Israeli Defence Forces.

Paras were again to the fore in the invasion of the Lebanon in 1982, and continued to be engaged in that unhappy country until the Israeli withdrawal. By this time there were five parachute brigades in the Israeli Defence Forces (IDF), and this is the situation today. Normally, two of these brigades are maintained at full strength, while the others can quickly be brought up to fighting order if necessary. Although the Israelis are notoriously (and understandably) secretive about the exact composition and disposition of their armed forces, it seems likely that within the paratroops there is a further, highly trained elite unit, Unit 269, which is in a constant state of readiness to deal with terrorist activities – men from this unit may well have carried out the Entebbe raid.

An honoured and indispensable part of their nation's armed forces they may now be, but in the beginning, Israel's paratroops were the subject of great controversy, and their early history illustrates just how difficult it is to create elite formations and units; for personal bravery, individual commitment and experience of being under fire are not enough on their own. A high level of technical skill and discipline is essential if a parachute corps is to be successful.

The Jewish settlers who came to what was then internationally known as Palestine during the early years of the 20th Century soon found themselves involved in conflict with the Palestinian Arabs, who saw no reason to accept that the land they had owned for centuries should be taken over by Jews – however strong the historical links of Judaism with the region and despite the fact that a substantial Jewish minority had continued to live in Palestine after the diaspora of the Jews

Above: Yitzhak Sadeh (centre), first commander of Palmach, with two of Israel's great soldiers: Moshe Dayan (left) and Yigal Allon.
Left: Yoel Palgi (left), the first commander of the Israeli Parachute Corps, with three comrades before their jump into Hungary to aid resistance groups during World War II.

during the Roman Empire. Conflict soon spilled over into violence, and both communities armed themselves for struggle – under the uneasy eye of the British authorities, who had ruled Palestine under a League of Nations mandate since the end of World War I.

There was regular, and recurring, violence during the 1930s; the 'Haganah' (Defence Force) came into being to protect Jewish settlements, and, on the advice of the British officer Orde Wingate (later to set up the Chindits who raided behind Japanese lines in World War II), the Jews formed 'Special Night Squads' that could act not only as defensive units, but also carry out reprisal or pre-emptive raids on Arab villages. By the outbreak of World War II, Jewish agitation for their own state in the land of Palestine was growing in intensity, fuelled by the mass persecution of Jews in German-controlled areas of Europe.

The attitude of the Jews in Palestine to the British during World War II was ambivalent. On the one hand, they condemned the British for not permitting more than a minimum of Jewish immigration into Palestine during the 1930s, and for refusing to offer them a state; on the other, they recognised that German victory in the war would have even

In 1920, Haganah ('Defence') was formed in response to anti-Jewish rioting in Jerusalem and northern Palestine. This organisation was a defensive workers' militia to protect Jewish settlements. Haganah had a difficult time at first; there was no real central command and arms were in very short supply. As a result, another outbreak of anti-Jewish rioting in 1929 resulted in heavy loss of life in some settlements and led to the formation of a National Command under the Jewish Agency (an umbrella organisation with representation from most Jewish groups in Palestine). A new campaign of Arab attacks on Jewish settlements began in 1936 but Haganah blunted many of these. The events of 1936 resulted in the formation of a number of units that would complement Haganah's defensive role by providing a strike force. Political disagreements between factions in Haganah led to the dissolution of the original group of strike companies in early 1939, but later that same year they were re-formed as Palmach ('Shock Force'). Palmach was a voluntary organisation and its tactics emphasised surprise, mobility and alertness. Commanders were expected to be amongst the first in attack and the last to withdraw, and were trained to close quickly with the enemy so that the fight would be at short ranges. By December 1947, when serious fighting broke out between Jews and Arabs in Palestine, there were about 45,000 members of Haganah, including 4000 well-armed Palmach fighters.

more disastrous consequences for them than for any other people. A Jewish Brigade fought with the British Army in the Mediterranean theatre, and two Jewish 'special units' were trained – although neither was particularly successful.

The first of these Jewish special units was one that consisted of German-born Jews, trained by two former members of the German Army, and designed to act behind Axis lines in North Africa. Unfortunately, on their first raid, against a German petrol dump near Tobruk, the Jewish commandos made little impression, and the unit was not re-formed.

The British put some Romanian and Hungarian Jews through a parachute course

More significant was the training of a group of Jewish volunteers later in the war to drop behind German lines in eastern Europe. The British were reluctant to agree to this scheme but eventually they put some Romanian and Hungarian Jews through a parachute course; two of those chosen were women. The Jewish interest was, of course, to try to rescue some of the east European Jews who had managed to avoid the concentration camps; the British wanted to rescue downed aircrew.

Above: Two Palmach men climb over a wall during the fighting in 1948.

Right: An infantryman of Palmach. The *ad hoc* nature of the fighting forces available to the newly-independent Israel meant they displayed little uniformity. This man wears a khaki drill shirt (probably of US origin) and British khaki drill trousers. The cartridge belt is a US design dating from World War I, and the water bottle is carried in a US World War II canteen cover. Armament consists of a 7.92mm Model 24 rifle, probably supplied from Czechoslovakia.

11

When the Jewish volunteers parachuted into Hungary, they met immediate disaster. They had been betrayed, and were captured by the Gestapo. The leader of one group was one of the women trainees, Hannah Szenes. Shortly before she was shot (after days of torture) she wrote a poem that has become almost a creed for Israeli paratroops. It ends:

'Blessed is the heart with strength to stop beating for the sake of honour,

'Blessed is the match consumed while kindling flame.'

Even before World War II came to an end, Jewish extremist groups dissatisfied with minimal British concessions had decided to take up the struggle directly against the British authorities, and a spiral of violence began to develop. Although there was considerable disquiet among the more moderate Jews at the activities of two terrorist groups, the Irgun and LEHI, which began to attack British forces in Palestine, the main Jewish military organisation, the Haganah, and its most highly trained section, the Palmach, were also prepared to carry the fight for a Jewish state to the point of attacking British installations.

While the fight against the British gained momentum, so did the struggle against the Palestinian Arabs. This came to a head after the British decided to renounce their mandate for Palestine; for the newly formed United Nations Organization

Below: A Haganah member changes the magazine on his comrade's Czech-supplied machine gun.
Right: Israeli troops on patrol near the Gaza Strip in 1955. The men of Unit 101 had gained their fearsome reputation during raids and patrols into and around the Gaza Strip and the West Bank.

Ben-Gurion's proclamation of the State of Israel on 14 May 1948 (above) was the final step in the rebirth of a Jewish state in Palestine. The growth of Zionism – a movement seeking a Jewish national homeland – in the late nineteenth century led to steady Jewish immigration to Palestine. This continued erratically until the 1930s, despite Arab opposition. The British, who since 1920 had held a League of Nations mandate for Palestine, were also unenthusiastic about immigration. The problem was exacerbated after 1945, when large numbers of refugees wished to leave Europe. The British authorities found it impossible to cope with Jewish–Arab antagonism, and submitted the problem to the United Nations in 1947. A commission resolved to partition Palestine into Arab and Jewish states, but by December 1947 there was almost open warfare between Jew and Arab in Palestine. After the declaration of a Jewish state in May 1948, the surrounding Arab states joined in the conflict, and fighting continued intermittently until a January 1949 cease-fire led to a series of armistices between Israel and her Arab neighbours.

agreed to partition the country between the two groups. There was more or less outright war in the period before the State of Israel was due to be proclaimed, and when it officially came into being in May 1948, the neighbouring Arab states combined in an invasion that they hoped would crush the fledgling nation – the Arab-Israeli wars had begun.

The first Israeli parachute unit was formed during this War of Independence

The first Israeli parachute unit was formed during this War of Independence. Yoel Palgi, the only survivor from the group that had parachuted into Hungary during World War II (he had been captured with the rest, but had leapt from the train carrying him to a concentration camp, and later made his way back to Palestine), was given the rank of major and the task of establishing a trained force. All the Israeli units that fought in this war faced the most formidable difficulties in acquiring enough equipment to prepare themselves for full-scale hostilities; and Israel was fortunate that its Arab enemies were riven with differences and mutually suspicious. The Jewish forces were highly motivated – many of them had personal experience of the Holocaust, and they were determined that such a disaster should never happen again. Many also had experience of small-scale warfare and knew about handling weapons, while some had served in the

13

Above: Meir Har-Zion, one of the heroes of Unit 101. Har-Zion was a skilful leader of men, and was promoted to captain despite the fact that he had never attended an officers' training course. Moshe Dayan regarded Har-Zion as Israel's best soldier.

British Army. With the aid of a small quantity of support weapons – heavy machine guns, a few aircraft and artillery pieces – the hastily thrown together Israeli forces were able to stop the Arab armies, and to force an armistice.

Paratroops played only a small role in this fight, however. For them, the lack of equipment was absolutely crippling. They had just one transport plane capable of carrying paras, and were forced to buy 4000 surplus British parachutes that were already on their way to a shirt factory. Many of these were sub-standard – and accidents in training soon reached an alarming level.

In addition to the lack of adequate equipment, the unit also suffered from a lack of the right sort of personnel. Bravery, commitment, skill with a gun were the raw material of ground troops – but parachuting requires, in addition, a skill that has to be taught. Some troops went on a training course in Czechoslovakia, but the training came too late for them to contribute to the war of 1948–49.

In 1949, Palgi resigned; his parachute unit had been relatively unsuccessful, and the high command was considering disbanding it. Instead of taking this step, however, they appointed a new commander, Yehuda Harari. Harari realised that discipline and sound training must replace the *ad hoc* methods of the early days. He introduced a rigorous training course and put his considerable energies into creating a new spirit. He also got more effective equipment – better parachutes, more aircraft.

Meanwhile, the Israelis were still fighting an undercover war against raiders from across the borders – and were initiating pre-emptive raids themselves. In 1953, a special force, Unit 101, was set up under Ariel Sharon, a former company commander in the 1948 War. Sharon's unit distinguished itself in the business of fighting secretly, at night, in hostile territory, and in some of these raids the men of Unit 101 were accompanied by Harari's paratroops.

The paratroops were now a far cry from the disorganised, barely trained, poorly equipped unit that had come out of the 1948 War. Their matchless commitment to fighting for the State of Israel was now tempered by the military discipline and know-how essential to the demanding techniques of airborne warfare. The high command therefore took the decision to amalgamate the men of Unit 101 with the paratroops, forming Unit 202. The command of this unit was given to Ariel Sharon of Unit 101 – something that Harari felt as a personal disappointment and he resigned as a result. But it was he who had created the firm, disciplined foundations that were the basis of 20 years of unchecked success.

Sharon introduced a new tactical approach into his unit, based upon speed and stealth rather than heavy covering fire, and Unit 202 soon became a byword for aggression and effective fighting qualities. It was encouraged by the new chief of staff, Moshe Dayan, who took over the IDF in 1953, and in 1955 Sharon's force was expanded into the 202nd Parachute Brigade, which was soon to be blooded in outright war during the Sinai Campaign of 1956.

1

ADVANCE INTO DANGER
Paras in the Mitla Pass

Previous page: An Israeli paratrooper lands in the desert. Below: Final preparations before the beginning of Operation Kadesh, the 1956 Israeli invasion of Sinai; men check their parachutes before boarding one of the 16 Dakotas earmarked for the drop. The venerable Dakota had been used during World War II by both British and US airborne forces.

1659 HOURS, 29 October 1956. Sixteen DC-3 Dakotas of the Israeli Air Force (IAF) skimmed low over the sun-baked hills of western Sinai, evading Egyptian radar surveillance. Above them, 10 Gloster Meteor jet fighters rode shotgun, their pilots keeping a wary eye peeled for enemy interceptors while, to the west, 12 Dassault Mystère IVA fighters patrolled the length of the Suez Canal. Inside the Dakotas, with only the monotonous drone of the aircraft engines to keep their thoughts from straying to the probable dangers they would face in a deep-penetration raid behind enemy lines, 395 men of the 1st Battalion of the newly-formed Israeli 202nd Parachute Brigade made their final preparations. Parachute harnesses and weapons, including the relatively untried Uzi sub-machine gun, were checked.

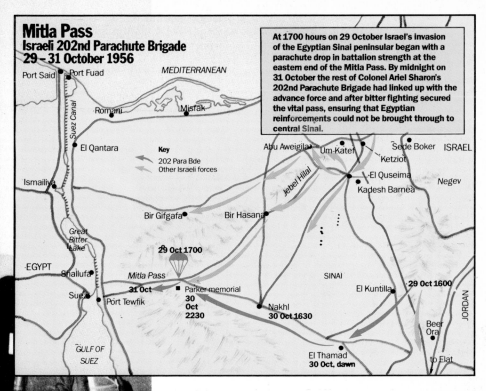

Mitla Pass
Israeli 202nd Parachute Brigade
29 – 31 October 1956

At 1700 hours on 29 October Israel's invasion of the Egyptian Sinai peninsular began with a parachute drop in battalion strength at the eastern end of the Mitla Pass. By midnight on 31 October the rest of Colonel Ariel Sharon's 202nd Parachute Brigade had linked up with the advance force and after bitter fighting secured the vital pass, ensuring that Egyptian reinforcements could not be brought through to central Sinai.

Key
202 Para Bde
Other Israeli forces

The battalion's commander, Lieutenant-Colonel Rafael 'Raful' Eitan, a battle-scarred veteran of many border clashes with the Arabs, was keenly aware of the importance of this drop on the strategically vital Mitla Pass, and he prayed that the scheduled link-up with the rest of the brigade, travelling overland under the command of Colonel Ariel 'Arik' Sharon, would take place before the Egyptians could respond to their landing. Moments later, however, the time for reflection was over; the aircraft climbed to 1500ft and, once at that altitude, Eitan led his men into the unknown. The pilots had done their job and now it was the turn of the paratroopers. Phase 1 of Operation Kadesh was under way.

Kadesh was the codename for the Israeli invasion of Sinai, to precede and provide the pretext for Anglo-French air and seaborne landings in the strategically vital Suez Canal Zone. All the parties concerned were trying to unseat Egyptian leader Gamal Abdel Nasser, whose aggressive brand of Arab nationalism ran contrary to British and French interests in the Middle East, and posed a threat to the very existence of the State of Israel.

The political background to the seizure of the Mitla Pass, the defile through which the main road to central Sinai ran, did not concern Eitan as he parachuted down to the drop zone. He, like any experienced commander, was considering the chances of success. Although his young charges had

17

Below: The Israelis arrive at the
Mitla Pass after a 200km journey
over enemy territory.
Below far right: The 202nd
Brigade digs in at the Mitla Pass.
The lack of natural cover made
unprotected troops very
vulnerable to strafing attacks by
enemy aircraft.

received the finest training the Israeli Defence Forces (IDF) could provide and exuded an air of casual confidence both in themselves and their officers, Eitan was acutely aware that this mission was their first large-scale operation and that its outcome depended on the reception they received on landing.

If the pre-drop preparations had gone according to plan, his paratroopers should land unopposed at the Parker Memorial, a local landmark lying on a rocky outcrop at the eastern end of the pass. Surprise was the key to success. To

ensure the maximum disruption of Egyptian communications and delay any response they might try to mount, four P-51 Mustangs of the IAF, flying at a hair-raising 4m above the ground, had cut overhead telegraph lines with their propellers before the drop took place.

Eitan hit the ground and rolled over, expecting the worst. To his surprise, the area was clear of the enemy. The landing, however, was not entirely unobserved; a motley group of Egyptian workers appeared and, believing the Israelis to be Egyptians, applauded their skilful descent and then offered the paratroopers mugs of coffee. The discovery that they had landed 5km from the target was a less welcome surprise. Time being of the essence, Eitan gathered his command and marched them to the eastern end of the pass which, after a brief firefight with a few Egyptian sentries, was captured. The paratroopers dug in and then settled down to await the arrival of their heavy equipment under Sharon.

Sharon's force, consisting of the other two battalions of the 202nd Brigade, two battalions of half-tracks, 13 AMX-13 tanks, a battery of 25pdrs and a heavy mortar company, had left its base on the Jordanian border a few hours before Eitan's departure and, although they had travelled across the Negev desert at breakneck speed, they crossed into Sinai 18 minutes behind schedule. Sharon knew that the outcome of the operation depended on meticulous timing, and he drove his men forward with redoubled vigour towards their first objective, the frontier post at El Kuntilla.

Rafael Eitan (above), one of Israel's most renowned soldiers, was born in 1929 at Tel Adashim, near Nazareth. He joined Palmach at the age of 17, and served as a deputy company commander in the 1948 War, when he was wounded at the battle of Katamon. He joined the paratroopers in 1950, and was commended for his role at the battle of Kunitla in 1955. In 1964 he became commander of the 202nd Brigade and was promoted to brigadier-general in 1968, when he became Chief Paratrooper and Infantry Officer. In 1973, as a major-general, he commanded a division on the Golan Heights. Between 1978 and 1983 he was Chief of the General Staff, with the rank of lieutenant-general. He retired from the army in 1983 and entered the Knesset, Israel's parliament, in 1984, as a member of a nationalist conservative party.

Above: An M3 half-track of Sharon's force drives into Sinai. Ahead lay a tough journey that was to include three lightning attacks against enemy positions.

The leading elements of the column arrived outside the post at 1600 on 29 October. There was no time for fancy planning or protracted combat – El Kuntilla had to be taken in minutes rather than hours. Sharon quickly appraised the situation and then unleashed two companies, travelling in machine-gun armed half-tracks, to the west of the Egyptian positions. With the benefit of the sun setting behind their backs, these men charged the enemy with guns blazing, while a handful of tanks and a single howitzer pounded the defenders who, blinded by the sun, were unable to pinpoint the Israeli attack. The ferocity of the assault was too much for the Egyptians, who fled into the desert. The battle was a morale-boosting success, but Sharon did not allow his men the luxury of self-congratulation. Instead, he goaded them to their next target, El Thamad, 60km to the west.

Below: French-supplied AMX-13s of the Israeli Defence Forces move across desert in the Sinai peninsula; Sharon's column had 13 of these tanks.

Right: An Israeli paratrooper at Mitla Pass. Eitan's command landed five kilometres from the eastern end of the pass, and had to march across desert to reach their objective. They brushed aside light opposition and then dug in to await the arrival of Sharon's column.

Sharon knew that this outpost would be a tougher nut to crack; intelligence reports had indicated that two Sudanese companies equipped with machine guns and recoilless rifles had strengthened the position's natural defences, a rock-strewn escarpment, with minefields and barbed wire. The Israelis arrived at dawn on the 30th with the sun at their backs, and launched an immediate attack. While two tanks opened up on the more visible enemy positions and laid a smoke screen, Aharon Davidi's battalion of paratroopers drove their half-tracks into the heart of the Sudanese defences. Once again, the élan of the Israeli attack, and the firepower they deployed, proved too much for the enemy, who fled, leaving 50 dead and their equipment behind. Israeli losses were light: four killed and six wounded.

Although his column had been on the move for the greater part of a day and had fought two large skirmishes, Sharon could ill afford any further delay. The Mitla Pass was still over 135km distant and the Egyptians, having recovered from their surprise at the attack, were closing in. But his men were exhausted and many of their vehicles were showing signs of wear and tear. Sharon had to order a halt.

A few hours after dawn, the advance recommenced and, after brushing aside a strafing attack by enemy jets, the Israelis reached Nakhl, the headquarters of an Egyptian

Ariel Sharon, the driving force behind the occupation of the Mitla Pass in 1956, was a controversial figure, who was destined to become a legend in the IDF. Sharon's rise to prominence began in the early 1950s when he was given the task of raising a specialist commando force, known as Unit 101, to carry out cross-border raids against Jordanian targets. Unit 101 rapidly established itself as a first-rate combat force and set the standards by which other IDF troops were judged. In 1954 Unit 101 and the paratroopers were integrated and, under the direction of Sharon, distinguished themselves in a series of retaliatory raids.

In the Six-Day War of 1967, Sharon led an armoured division in the Sinai desert and played a key role in the defeat of the Egyptian 2nd Division at Abu Aweigila. It was in the Yom Kippur War of 1973, however, that Sharon's heavy-handed independence brought him into direct confrontation with his fellow officers. He was accused of disobeying orders and there were calls for his resignation. He was also fiercely criticised in 1982 when, as Defence Minister, he masterminded the invasion of Lebanon (Operation Peace for Galilee). In the wake of the massacre of Palestinians by Christian militiamen, he resigned his post.

frontier force battalion, at 1630 hours on the 30th. Barely pausing to assess the situation, Sharon launched a head-on charge backed by an artillery barrage, but the garrison fled before battle could be joined. At 1700 the Israelis entered the village, swapped some of their battered trucks for the Soviet-built BTR 152 armoured personnel carriers left in the compound and then drove off towards Mitla, 65km to the west.

The fire and dash that had carried him through the desert proved to be Sharon's undoing

The fall of Nakhl assured the success of the Israeli plan and, despite the strain that the final lap of the journey placed on both men and machines, Sharon linked up with Eitan at 2230 hours. In a truly remarkable drive that owed much to the indomitable personality and dogged determination of Sharon, the column had travelled through 200km of inhospitable, enemy-held territory in less than 32 hours.

The situation at the pass, however, was considerably less secure than either Eitan or Sharon believed. Although the paratroopers had spotted Egyptian aircraft in their vicinity, they remained unaware that the response to their incursion was gathering momentum. On the morning of 30 October, the Egyptians had dispatched the 2nd Brigade from Suez to confront the Israelis and, despite heavy attacks launched by the IAF, the brigade's 5th Battalion and a company of the 6th reached the area.

At Mitla, the road from Suez meanders through a sheer-sided 32km-long defile that is little more than 50m wide. Unbeknown to the Israelis, the Egyptians had taken up position in and around some caves on the Jebel Heitan that lay along the southern edge of the road, and in dug-outs along a ridge to the north. Their defences bristled with heavy machine guns, 12 6pdr anti-tank guns and dozens of Alpha light machine guns.

Although unaware of the Egyptian occupation of the pass, Sharon recognised that his paratroopers were dangerously over-exposed and, in view of their vulnerability to air attack, he sought to move deeper into the pass. After discussing the matter with Lieutenant-General Moshe Dayan, the Israeli Chief of Staff, he received permission to send out a small patrol to reconnoitre the ground on condition that they avoid large-scale combat. The fire and dash that had carried him through the desert now proved to be Sharon's undoing. Despite Dayan's explicit orders, he dispatched two reinforced companies under Mordechai 'Motta' Gur into the defile.

Gur's force motored into Mitla, blithely unaware of the Egyptian presence in the caves on either side of the track. Coolly, the enemy waited until the leading Israeli vehicles were well inside their prepared killing grounds. As the column rounded a sharp bend, the leading half-track was met by a devastating fusillade. The driver and his commander fell, riddled with bullets, and their vehicle skidded

Above: Four of the Israeli Defence Forces' most renowned soldiers meet at the Mitla Pass. From the right: Rafael Eitan, Ariel Sharon, Danny Matt; second from left: Mordechai Gur.

Left: An Israeli Air Force P-51 flies over the paratroops at the Mitla Pass. The Israelis had achieved air superiority over Sinai by 31 October.

Above: A member of the 202nd Brigade after the end of the Sinai campaign.

across the path of the following trucks. Undaunted, Gur pressed on, believing the opposition to be light. He was quickly disillusioned; his own half-track was hit by a well-aimed anti-tank round and its dazed crew was forced to shelter in a ditch.

The blazing wreckage of the leading vehicles, however, did not halt the Israelis' progress. The rest of Gur's men drove on, their guns blazing away indiscriminately, until they reached a saucer-shaped depression in the middle of the pass, where they were forced to halt. By 1300 hours, the whole column was pinned down by sustained fire.

Sharon ordered Davidi, one of his most trusted officers and the victor of El Thamad, to attempt the rescue of Gur's men. Recognising the futility of any further attempt to advance down the pass, he dispatched the brigade's reconnaissance company to a hill north of the visible Egyptian positions. As the company began its advance downhill, it was met by fierce fire from hitherto unseen enemy bunkers. The Israelis, unable to pinpoint the source of the withering fire, were forced to concede ground since any further advance would have been suicidal.

Davidi was forced to make a fateful decision; he asked for a volunteer to drive into the pass to draw the enemy's fire, thereby enabling his paratroopers to pinpoint the Egyptian positions. His call was answered by many brave men, including Eitan, but Davidi chose a young recruit for the task. Gathering an unarmoured jeep, the volunteer sped down the road into a deadly cross-fire. The driver, riddled with bullets, crashed his vehicle, but his sacrifice was not in vain. The enemy-held caves were noted.

As darkness fell, small groups of Israelis edged along the scree-slopes beneath the Egyptian emplacements. Carrying only sub-machine guns and plentiful supplies of hand grenades, the paratroopers crept into positions around the mouths of the caves. Then, they began their grim, bloody task. Grenades were lobbed and Uzis were fired; the noise of countless explosions rent the night air. For two-and-a-half hours the battle raged; neither side asked for quarter. One by one, the paratroopers took the enemy positions and, by midnight, the pass was firmly in Israeli hands. More than 260 Egyptians died that night. Later, the brigade regrouped and had a roll-call; they were shocked to find that they had lost 38 men killed and a further 120 wounded in an unnecessary action, brought about by Sharon's over-enthusiam. The brigade withdrew from the pass next morning and needed 48 hours' rest before it was fit for action again. Nevertheless, the battle allowed other Israeli columns to meet and defeat the Egyptians in northern Sinai.

Mitla Pass was a bloody debut for the 202nd Parachute Brigade. Faced with an ambush of such intensity, a lesser unit would have crumbled, but the training and courage of Sharon's men saved the day. The battle was the first of many tests that Israel's paratroopers would meet with skill and resolution.

2

PARAS UNDER FIRE
Fighting in the Gaza Strip

The immediate causes of the Six-Day War lay in the volatile internal politics of Israel's neighbours. During the early 1960s, Egypt's President Nasser sought to find a long-term solution, at a series of summits, to the question of the continued existence of Israel. The Arab nations could not agree on a strategy, however, and several states – most notably Saudi Arabia – were unhappy with Nasser's radical politics. After the foundation of the Palestine Liberation Organisation (PLO) at the 1964 First Arab Summit, Yasser Arafat's Al Fatah group, dedicated to a military solution to the situation, launched a series of guerrilla raids that prompted the Israelis into retaliatory cross-border actions. By 1967, the Syrians, who bore the brunt of Israel's response, asked Nasser for tangible military support. Nasser ordered the mobilisation of Egypt's armed forces, a measure that was enthusiastically received by the Egyptian people. During the latter part of May 1967 the Egyptians deployed in Sinai and requested the removal of the United Nations peacekeeping force which had manned observation posts along the Egyptian-Israeli border since 1956. A formal military alliance between Syria, Egypt and Jordan at the end of May led Israel to mobilise its reservists. This placed an immense strain on the Israeli economy and Israel's government ordered a pre-emptive strike to resolve the situation.

Page 25: Israeli paratroops scan nearby buildings for enemy snipers.
Right: The author of this chapter, Lieutenant-Colonel Rafael Eitan (right), in conference with General Israel Tal.
Far right: A column of paratroops in jeeps moves through the Gaza Strip.

DURING THE Six-Day War of June 1967 I had the honour of commanding the 202nd Parachute Brigade of the Israeli Defence Forces. One of the most outstanding and professional units in Israel's army, it was destined to play an important role in the battles to eject the Egyptians from the Gaza Strip and Sinai.

Tensions in the area had been building for some time before the war began, and both we and the Egyptians had been mobilising our troops. By the beginning of June, the Egyptian commander, General Abdel Mohsen Mortagui, had massed some 100,000 men and 950 tanks in Sinai. As our troops were completing their preparations for our offensive, codenamed Red Sheet, I discovered what role we would play in the action. As part of the force led by Major-General Israel Tal, my brigade was ordered to clear the Gaza Strip.

During the previous weeks, Mortagui had fed more troops into the Strip, and our intelligence services had identified Major-General Mohammed Hasni's 20th (Palestinian) Infantry Division and the 7th Infantry Division under Major-General Abdel Aziz Soliman in the area. The enemy had 150 Sherman, T34 and Josef Stalin III tanks to stiffen the defences.

Less than 12 hours before the start of the operation, on the evening of 4 June, I asked Major-General Tal to consider a last-minute change of strategy. I thought that my paratroopers should make a wide, sweeping attack around the southern edge of the enemy's defences at Rafah, and then head northwards to take their positions from the rear. Tal agreed to my suggestions and I was told to attack at the same time as the 7th Armoured Brigade, led by Colonel Shmuel Gonen,

In between the 1956 Sinai Campaign and the 1967 Six-Day War the Israeli Defence Forces (IDF) closely examined their operational techniques. This measure was given added emphasis by the wholesale re-equipment of their armoured units which took place at the same time. Some of Israel's military leaders – such as General Israel Tal – believed that the modern tank with air support would dominate the battlefield totally as massive tank units engaged in a large cross-country mêlée. Others – such as Moshe Dayan, who masterminded the 1956 campaign – believed that the IDF should rely on traditional combined arms units of tanks and mechanised infantry.

In practice, during the Six-Day War, the IDF's operations were closer to the 'combined arms' school than the 'dominant tank' view. General Ariel Sharon, in the fighting for Umm Katef, used helicopters, engineers and artillery in support of his tank and infantry strike force. Tanks were used to defeat enemy tanks. Infantry followed in the wake of the tanks, mopping up any remaining enemy troops.

Far right: Led by M50 Shermans, paratroopers in half-tracks begin the race for the Suez Canal.

made its move from the northeast, near the town of Khan Yunis.

After leaving the meeting I made my final dispositions. I had decided to attack in four groups: the reconnaissance troops in the lead; the paras following; and the 30 AMX-13 tanks of Colonel Amnon Reshef protecting the flanks. I placed the battalion HQ in the centre. I knew the fighting would be hard; the Egyptians had thrown two infantry brigades, lavishly backed by artillery, into the defence of Rafah, and had posted a company of Stalin tanks along the road to the south. All was ready.

I saw our jets streaking towards Sinai and knew that war had begun

Shortly before 0800 hours on 5 June, I saw our jets streaking towards Sinai and knew that the war had begun. Moments later, the order to start our attack, Red Sheet, was broadcast. The main problem I encountered during the advance was in trying to keep the different formations in order. One of the tank units diverted a little to the west of the planned route and ran into an Egyptian force. A tank was hit, but the black smoke rising from its shattered hull showed where we were to swing north behind the enemy's front line.

Striking the first Egyptian brigade side on, my right flank units met with fierce resistance from an enemy holding a series of heavily fortified trenches. The troops on the other flank, however, scythed through the poorly-held rear areas and quickly reached the road between Rafah and El Arish.

Meanwhile, I had taken up position with the brigade HQ in the middle of the battlefield. Suddenly, we found ourselves separated from the other troops and fighting for our lives against the enemy's rearguard, supported by artillery and mortars. I decided to inform the divisional commander of our progress and present situation. Holding a radio set in one hand and a sub-machine gun in the other, I informed him of our difficulties.

After hearing my report, punctuated by bursts of fire, he wanted to despatch an armoured unit to my aid. I told him that the crisis would pass and we would defeat the enemy without any further help. However, it took another two hours of vicious fighting before I was able to reform my force.

Once under control, I ordered the left flank force to join my HQ troops and then push towards the Rafah junction. This point was the northern edge of the enemy's defences, and by taking this objective I hoped to ease the pressure on my right flank force as it pushed up from the south. Between us lay over four kilometres of enemy-held territory.

Once at the junction, I established a communication base and radioed the commander of my southern force to get a clearer picture of the situation. He reported heavy casualties, adding that he also was wounded. We tried to evacuate the worst cases by helicopter. I knew that the battle rested on a knife edge and determined to reach the southern force at all costs.

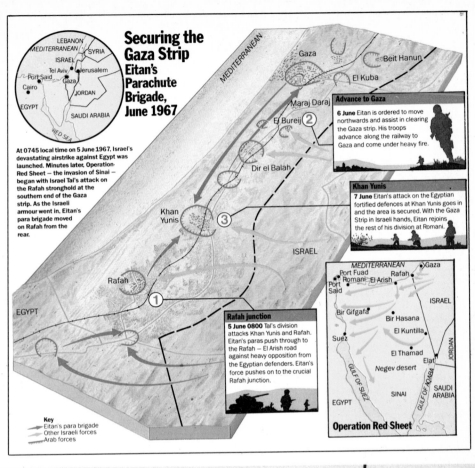

Securing the Gaza Strip
Eitan's Parachute Brigade, June 1967

At 0745 local time on 5 June 1967, Israel's devastating airstrike against Egypt was launched. Minutes later, Operation Red Sheet — the invasion of Sinai — began with Israel Tal's attack on the Rafah stronghold at the southern end of the Gaza strip. As the Israeli armour went in, Eitan's para brigade moved on Rafah from the rear.

Advance to Gaza

6 June Eitan is ordered to move northwards and assist in clearing the Gaza strip. His troops advance along the railway to Gaza and come under heavy fire.

Khan Yunis

7 June Eitan's attack on the Egyptian fortified defences at Khan Yunis goes in and the area is secured. With the Gaza Strip in Israeli hands, Eitan rejoins the rest of his division at Romani.

Rafah junction

5 June 0800 Tal's division attacks Khan Yunis and Rafah. Eitan's paras push through to the Rafah — El Arish road against heavy opposition from the Egyptian defenders. Eitan's force pushes on to the crucial Rafah junction.

Operation Red Sheet

Key
→ Eitan's para brigade
→ Other Israeli forces
⌇ Arab forces

The Egyptian Army of the 1967 War was the successor to a force founded by the British in their Egyptian protectorate in 1882. In the 1948 War with Israel this force performed in a lacklustre manner, hampered by an officer corps that was dominated by the sons of wealthy families.

Four years later radical-nationalist, middle-ranking officers took power in Egypt and, because of their opposition to Anglo-French economic dominance of the country, they began to look to other models for the Egyptian Army. An arms deal with Czechoslovakia, agreed in 1955, was followed by the war with Britain, France and Israel in 1956, which forced Egypt to turn to the Soviet Union and its Warsaw Pact allies for arms and military training. The Egyptian Army increased its stock of T34s and in the early 1960s received T54/55s.

The military establishment was also streamlined by the new regime: a Ministry of War Production was formed to develop the Egyptian arms industry, and a National Military Service Law was introduced in 1956, instituting selective service for all Egyptian men for a three-year term. By June 1967, the Egyptian Army totalled 160,000 men. The standard infantry rifle was the AK-47. There were over 1000 armoured fighting vehicles available (including T34s, T54/55s, JSIIIs and SU 100s) and there was also lavish artillery support provided.

After forming a plan, I called over the senior tank commander, and said: 'We will move with your tanks to the south, straight against the Egyptians and join our southern forces.' He answered: 'We only have enough fuel for one hour, and there are some tanks without ammunition.' I replied: 'We go! Tanks low on fuel will move as far as they can, and those without ammunition will not shoot.'

I jumped into the leading vehicle and the whole force, consisting of no more than five tanks, roared into action. The move was decisive. Despite heavy opposition, we reached our fellow paratroopers at sunset. As if by magic, hundreds of Egyptians left their trenches and fled to the west. We took many of these men prisoner and those who escaped were later caught by other units of Tal's division in the El Arish area. After clearing the area, we returned to the junction at Rafah to prepare for the next day's fighting. In fact, only one tank made it back; the rest ran out of fuel.

At nightfall, the various units of my command had taken up position at the junction and, though we were all exhausted, we worked until midnight. It was at this point that a young officer came forward to tell me that my nephew had been killed. Although the news was a sad blow, I could not show my true feelings to my men so I thanked the officer and went back to work.

It was during these hours that I learned the full story of the right flank force's fight. One of the stories I heard is carved in my memory. As the bitter fighting continued, our wounded were collected by medical personnel and treated in an abandoned trench. Suddenly, an enemy tank appeared from nowhere and bore down on the wounded. Only the medical orderlies were fit enough to fight the tank, and one of them lifted a bazooka, firing at the Stalin III when it was less than 10m away. The shell did not harm the monster, but the noise and impact were enough to force the Egyptians to leave the vehicle.

As we approached the town, the lead tank rolled over a mine and was disabled

On the morning of the 6th, I was ordered to leave Tal's armoured division and move my men north to help in clearing the enemy from the Gaza Strip. I was only given very general instructions and, as I had lost radio contact with headquarters, I decided on my own initiative to head north along a railway towards Khan Yunis. As we approached the town, the lead tank rolled over a mine and was disabled. I then moved out to the east of Khan Yunis to avoid any other unpleasant surprises and pressed on towards Gaza. However, one of my units mistakenly entered the town, and came under very heavy and well-directed fire. It would have been a blunder to leave a strong enemy force in our rear, so I resolved to clear Khan Yunis on the following day (7 June).

That night we parked along the main road to the east of the enemy's positions. We had had nothing to eat over the last two days but a quick search revealed several ducks. I was

Left: Members of a patrol march through a deserted town during a mopping-up operation.

Below: A pair of AMX-13s lead an Israeli column through the Gaza Strip. Eitan's men had the support of 30 AMX-13s under Colonel Amnon Reshef.

appointed chef. After the meal, we fell asleep in a convenient ditch. In the morning, my force was joined by two tanks that had developed mechanical problems during the earlier stages and had lost contact with their unit.

The attack on Khan Yunis went in as planned, and after a brief skirmish we captured key positions and smashed the enemy's will to resist. As the fighting died down, I received an urgent message warning me to expect an attack by enemy units moving down the coast from the north. I was somewhat taken aback by this information, as our troops were reported to have cleared the Gaza Strip the day before.

Through my binoculars I saw several tank guns turning in our direction

However, I decided to investigate the sighting and, after arranging a small force of jeeps and tanks, we headed north along the coast. About 2000m from the village of Dir-el-Balah our column halted and I searched the streets for signs of the enemy. Looking through my binoculars, I saw several tank guns turning, aiming in our direction. At the last moment, I realised that the 'enemy' was a force of Israeli tanks. Immediately, I ordered our tanks to turn and lower their guns in recognition, and the tanks in the village did the same. After verifying the situation, I moved my men back to Khan Yunis to await instructions.

Later in the morning, I received orders from Tal to move south along the coast and head for the Suez Canal. I was informed that an artillery unit was waiting in Romani to join my force.

I gathered my officers for a briefing and, as we were finalising our plans, several Israeli Mirage jets flew low overhead. I was able to contact the formation and discovered that its commanding officer was an old friend. Before the war we had agreed that, if I gave him a certain radio call, he would come to my aid. Using the pre-arranged signal, I asked him to fly towards the Suez Canal and search for signs of the enemy. Coming back after several minutes, he reported that there were Egyptians in the city of El Qantara and that his aircraft had destroyed three tanks with cannon fire. I thanked him for his help, and as a parting gesture I asked him to contact my wife to tell her I was well.

We finished all our preparations and I made my dispositions for the advance on El Qantara. With the command unit leading along the road, the jeeps were spread out along the left flank and the tanks and infantry were massed on the right. The troops would go in under a protective umbrella provided by 105mm artillery.

We soon made contact with the enemy. Looking to my left, I spied several Egyptian tanks massing against the jeeps. I immediately warned the commander and he, noting the location of the advancing tanks, organised a reception committee. Taken unawares, the enemy's tanks were dealt with by 106mm recoilless rifles. The action was so swift that we were soon moving forward on our objective.

Right: A severely wounded paratrooper, the victim of an Egyptian mine, is helped to safety by a comrade. The Egyptian and Palestinian forces defending the Gaza Strip relied heavily on fighting from strong defensive positions, and minefields were an important part of their arrangements.

Below: Israeli paratroopers take cover in the back of their half-track as an enemy sniper opens fire.

Above: Scenes of jubilation outside the town of El Arish at the end of the campaign. Israel's victory was absolute; up to 80 per cent of the enemy's forces in Sinai were destroyed as fighting units.

Looking to the right, I noticed the tell-tale mushroom of smoke that accompanies the firing of an anti-tank missile, and then saw the small red dot that marked its aiming point. Following it with my binoculars, I told my officers that the missile would pass over our vehicle. It did, but another then shattered a telephone post less than five metres from my position. Scanning the ground for the enemy, I saw several Egyptian soldiers lying in a ditch waiting to ambush my right flank units.

As I radioed a hurried warning, I was hit by enemy fire and sank to the floor of my armoured vehicle, trying to keep a firm grip on a metal bar. I knew that I was seriously wounded and remember hearing other officers calling for medics. I was laid on the ground and received expert attention while my men silenced the enemy.

I was unable to talk easily, but I signalled for some shade and whispered the name of the officer to take over the command. A little later, I was evacuated by helicopter. After reaching El Arish, I was transferred to a larger aircraft and flown to the hospital at Beersheba. My part in the Six-Day War was over.

Despite losing their commanding officer, my paratroopers stuck to the task. The Egyptian forces at El Qantara were smashed and on the fourth day of the war (8 June) 202nd Para reached the banks of the Suez Canal. Two days later the war was over, and Sinai was firmly under our control. The paratroopers had played their part in our sweeping victory. The Egyptian armed forces were shattered: over 10,000 men had been killed, 20,000 wounded and 5500 captured; some 500 tanks were destroyed and 300 captured; 450 artillery pieces and 10,000 other vehicles were also taken. Our losses were remarkably light: 275 killed and 800 wounded.

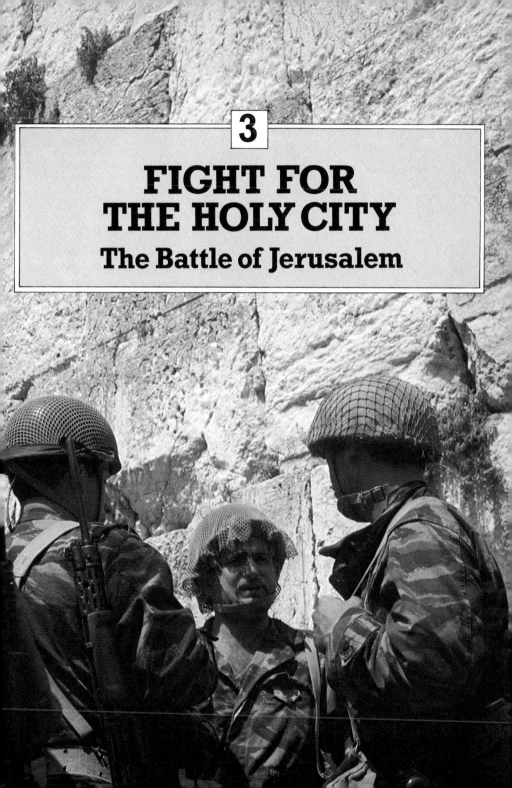

3

FIGHT FOR
THE HOLY CITY

The Battle of Jerusalem

JERUSALEM AND ISRAEL

Throughout the pre-Christian era, the city of Jerusalem was the site of the Temple, the holiest shrine of the Jewish religion. The structure was magnificently rebuilt during the reign of King Herod at the end of the first century BC, after Rome had imposed its rule on the whole of the eastern Mediterranean. However, after Roman imperial policy provoked a Jewish nationalist uprising, Herod's Temple was destroyed in AD 70. All that remained was one wall – the Western (Wailing) Wall – which was incorporated into the city walls of Jerusalem. Another revolt in AD 135 resulted in a decree that prohibited Jews from living in the Holy City.

For the next 1700 years, the majority of the Jewish people were scattered throughout the Middle East, Europe and North Africa. Despite this, they kept alive the memory of their homeland in the Jewish liturgy and in rabbinical writings.

In the late 19th Century the Zionist movement, aiming to secure a Jewish homeland in Palestine, became the dominant political force among Jews the world over. But even after this dream was realised in 1948, that part of Jerusalem which contained the Wailing Wall remained out of Israel, for the Old City was under Jordanian control.

Page 35: Israeli paratroopers stand beside the Wailing Wall after the battle.

SHORTLY AFTER 0930 hours on the morning of Wednesday, 7 June 1967, Colonel Mordechai Gur, commander of the 55th Parachute Brigade, spoke on the radio net to his waiting paratroopers:

'We stand on a ridge overlooking the Holy City. Soon we will enter the city, the Old City of Jerusalem about which countless generations of Jews have dreamed, to which all living Jews aspire. To our brigade has been granted the privilege of being the first to enter it.'

The capture of Jerusalem was the most potent symbol of Jewish victory in the Six-Day War of 1967, for the control of the Holy Places, such as the Temple Mount and the Wailing Wall, was enormously important to the young state of Israel. The honour of being the troops who would physically take possession of this great prize had been earned by Gur's men, who had shown great courage and skill over the past two days. In particular, they had wrested control of northern Jerusalem from the experienced and well dug-in forces of the Jordanian Army in the early morning of 6 June.

Tension had been building between Israel and her Arab neighbours for some time when, on the morning of 5 June, the Israeli Air Force launched a sudden strike against the Egyptians. This was totally successful, but in the confusion of that morning's events, King Hussein of Jordan was led to believe that the Israelis had themselves been hard hit, and agreed to send his forces in to attack Israel. At 1100 hours a bombardment began from the Jordanian side of the heavily fortified border, and the Jordanian Air Force flew sorties into Israeli air space. This was a foolhardy move that Hussein was to regret bitterly. Within hours, the rampant Israelis had put his entire air force out of action, and Major-General Uzi Narkiss, in charge of Central Command, was putting into operation his contingency plans for an offensive against Jordanian territory.

The 16th Jerusalem Brigade cut the main Jordanian communications

The Israelis had to cope with an unpromising strategic situation. Their main problem was that a long, narrow finger of land, inviting attack or artillery barrage from the Jordanian territory on either side, was the only link with the Israeli-held areas of Jerusalem. This corridor had to be made secure, and so Narkiss used the tanks of Colonel Ben Ari's 10th Mechanised Brigade to push north of the corridor and seize the ridge linking Jerusalem with the important centre of Ramallah; at the same time, Latrun was attacked and overrun. Meanwhile, to the south of the corridor, the 16th Jerusalem Brigade launched a series of attacks that cut the main Jordanian communications with their forces in Hebron. The success of these two sets of operations, greatly helped by the command of the air that the Israeli Air Force was now exerting, gave the situation a new complexion.

Within Jerusalem, the possibilities and prospects for either side were complicated by two factors. First, there was

Taking the West Bank

MEDITERRANEAN

Jenin
Nablus
Tubas
Tel Aviv
Ramallah
Ashdod
Jerusalem
Jericho
Ashkelon
Bethlehem
Gaza
WEST BANK
Hebron
DEAD SEA
ISRAEL
JORDAN
Jordan

The road to Jerusalem

JORDAN
ISRAEL
Sha'alvim
Beth Haron Pass
Ramallah
Latrun
Radar Hill
Bidu
Atarot
Maale Hahamisha
Police School
Mount Scopus
Kastel
Motza
Mount of Olives
Sheikh Jarrah
Jerusalem
UN HQ

Key
Israeli forces
Arab forces
Israeli enclave
Arab enclave

Battle for Jerusalem
Israeli 55th Parachute Brigade, June 1967

At 1100 hours on 5 June 1967 Jordanian artillery and aircraft began attacking targets in Israel. Faced with the problem of defending the corridor to Jerusalem against a Jordanian advance, the Israelis deployed an armoured brigade to secure the high ground north of the corridor. With the northern flank secure the 55th Parachute Brigade began its attack on Jerusalem, entering the Old City early on 7 June. Meanwhile, Israeli forces were clearing the rest of the West Bank, and that evening hostilities between Israel and Jordan ended.

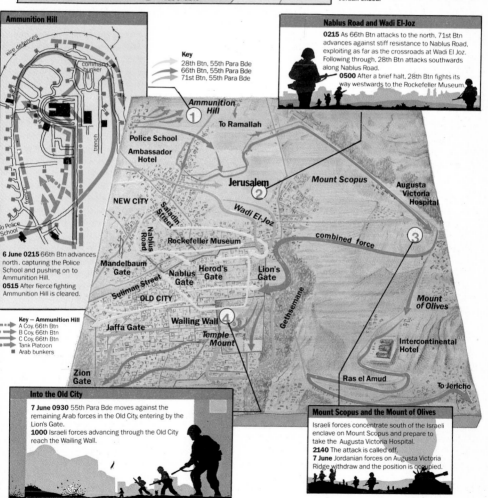

Ammunition Hill

wire defences
command bunker
trench
To Police School

6 June 0215 66th Btn advances north, capturing the Police School and pushing on to Ammunition Hill.
0515 After fierce fighting Ammunition Hill is cleared.

Key – Ammunition Hill
A Coy, 66th Btn
B Coy, 66th Btn
C Coy, 66th Btn
Tank Platoon
Arab bunkers

Key
28th Btn, 55th Para Bde
66th Btn, 55th Para Bde
71st Btn, 55th Para Bde

Ammunition Hill
To Ramallah
Police School
Ambassador Hotel
Jerusalem
NEW CITY
Mount Scopus
Augusta Victoria Hospital
Saladin Street
Wadi El-Joz
combined force
Nablus Road
Rockefeller Museum
Mandelbaum Gate
Nablus Gate
Herod's Gate
Lion's Gate
Suliman Street
OLD CITY
Gethsemane
Mount of Olives
Jaffa Gate
Wailing Wall
Temple Mount
Intercontinental Hotel
Zion Gate
Ras el Amud
To Jericho

Nablus Road and Wadi El-Joz

0215 As 66th Btn attacks to the north, 71st Btn advances against stiff resistance to Nablus Road, exploiting as far as the crossroads at Wadi El Joz. Following through, 28th Btn attacks southwards along Nablus Road.
0500 After a brief halt, 28th Btn fights its way westwards to the Rockefeller Museum.

Into the Old City

7 June 0930 55th Para Bde moves against the remaining Arab forces in the Old City, entering by the Lion's Gate.
1000 Israeli forces advancing through the Old City reach the Wailing Wall.

Mount Scopus and the Mount of Olives

Israeli forces concentrate south of the Israeli enclave on Mount Scopus and prepare to take the Augusta Victoria Hospital.
2140 The attack is called off.
7 June Jordanian forces on Augusta Victoria Ridge withdraw and the position is occupied.

a substantial Israeli enclave within Jordanian territory on Mount Scopus, comprising the Hadassah Hospital and the Hebrew University. A prime Israeli goal was to relieve this enclave (which had been maintained, under United Nations auspices, since 1948) while the Jordanians in turn wished to overrun the position. The second factor affecting operations in the city was that in the two decades since the establishment of the existing frontier, both sides had built up complex sets of fortifications. These networks of deep concrete bunkers, carefully-sited linking trenches, mines and barbed wire made a frontal offensive difficult, if not impossible.

The main Jordanian force in the city was the 27th Infantry Brigade, under Brigadier Ata Ali. Further brigades were in support to both north and south, while a tank battalion was stationed behind the main built-up areas in the Kidron valley. The Israeli Air Force made every effort to cut the communication lines of these forces with the Jordanian concentrations further to the north and east, but Ali was a competent officer and he had been reinforced. His men, basically the former Arab Legion under a different name, were well trained and confident of the strength of their defensive positions. Against them, the Israelis decided to throw in one of their crack formations – the 55th Parachute Brigade.

The paras would have to fight their way through an awesome set of obstacles

The 55th Parachute Brigade was a body of men trained to expect shock action and to be in the forefront of any Israeli offensive. Under its experienced commander, Colonel Mordechai Gur, were many veterans of raids on Arab territory, although some of the most senior officers had not yet seen action. Raised to a fever pitch by the days of waiting before the air strike that marked the beginning of the Six-Day War, the paras had expected to be used against the Egyptians in Sinai, and at noon on the 5th were told to prepare for a jump against El Arish, to give impetus to the northern axis of advance. However, such was the pace of the Israeli success that by 1600 hours the decision was taken to use the whole brigade against the Jordanians in Jerusalem.

The basic plan was for the 66th and 71st Battalions of the 55th Brigade to attack along a front running from the Mandelbaum Gate to a point opposite the Jordanian-held Police School building. When a breakthrough had been made, the 28th Battalion would push through to exploit southwards, towards the walls of the Old City. Some support would come from the tanks attached to the Jerusalem Brigade, but the paras would have to fight their way through an awesome set of obstacles with only minimum support before the attack could gather momentum.

The staff of the 55th Brigade urgently prepared for the assault. It was due to go in as soon as possible, but in the event, the battalions would not be ready before 0215 hours

BANGALORE TORPEDOES

In 1912 trials were held at Bangalore in India to discover effective methods of breaching barbed-wire entanglements. One device was the invention of Captain McClintock of the Indian Sappers and Miners. His torpedo consisted of a 5.5m length of water piping stuffed with 27kg of dynamite, and it was so successful that the spectators only narrowly escaped being blown up with the wire.

Modified versions of McClintock's weapon were widely used by sappers in the trenches during World War I, but since then its use has declined. A typical modern Bangalore torpedo consists of a 1.8m light steel tube, 38mm in diameter, packed with 1.8kg of ammonal blasting explosive. Fitted with spring-locking clips at both ends, individual tubes are locked together to form a long charge that penetrates to the far side of the obstacle. The head of the torpedo is streamlined by a smooth, conical nose that helps to prevent the weapon snagging on the wire as it is pushed in. Once slid into position, the connected tubes of the torpedo are fired by an electric detonator fixed to the end of the final section.

The Israeli paratroops in Jerusalem linked up the sections and then carried them forward, one man to a section, to the wire. But there were several problems: for example, if a man stumbled or was hit by shrapnel, sections would come apart and had to be hastily reassembled.

Far left, top: Men of the 55th Brigade loading equipment for the aborted jump at El Arish. Far left: Mordechai Gur (using radio) with paratroopers on the Mount of Olives.

Fight for the Holy City

Right: Israeli paratroopers advance on one of the gates of the Old City.

Main picture: In front of the historic site of the Garden of Gethsemane, Israeli paratroopers shelter from Jordanian sniper fire.

on the 6th. The crews manning the 81mm mortars were especially concerned, because the shells they needed were very slow in arriving. They were anxious to start rangefinding, but could not risk running short of ammunition. Units were getting lost as they struggled to find their place in the line and Jordanian shells, falling at random, were causing casualties. But eventually, at 0215 on 6 June, the barrage began.

With buildings on the Jordanian side bursting into flame and lines of tracer flicking through the darkness, the first Israeli platoons approached the Jordanian positions. They thrust Bangalore torpedoes below the coils of barbed wire, and then hastily pulled back and hit the deck. The 71st Battalion in particular had trouble in their sector: Bangalore torpedoes were not exploding, and then further wire obstacles were looming up after the first breach had been made. The delays meant that men moving forward to exploit the expected breach caused overcrowding, and the milling soldiers could have been very vulnerable to Jordanian shells. Eventually the way through was cleared. Waving green torches (usually the recognition signal for assembly after a night jump) to indicate that the path was open, officers led the platoons through into the next phase of the assault.

Once through the wire, the 66th Battalion was to exploit northwards, through the Police School, taking the important position of Ammunition Hill, while the 71st Battalion was to move through the Sheikh Jarrah area and the American Colony towards the Wadi El-Joz. The men of the 66th knew that they would face enormous difficulties. Ammunition Hill was a vital point, and the Police School itself was well fortified. The paras were heavily laden, carrying extra magazines for their Uzi sub-machine guns and knapsacks stuffed with grenades. In some cases, men were unable to get up when they fell over, and in one narrow trench Israeli troops got stuck because they were too bulky to pass along.

Explosions of tank, mortar and 25pdr shells provided a deadly backdrop

Giant searchlights illuminated the white walls of the Police School; Jordanian flares suddenly lit up the whole scene. Blazing houses made the darkness around them seem even darker, and the constant explosions of tank, mortar and Jordanian 25pdr shells provided a deadly backdrop as the paras pushed ahead. It was impossible to see exactly where the enemy smallarms fire was coming from.

First into the Police School was A Company, cutting a way through a cattle-fence outside. The long passages inside were completely dark, a darkness rendered even more impenetrable by the sudden shell flashes outside. Groups of four men cleared the rooms, two throwing in a grenade and then spraying a room with fire, while the other two moved on to the room next door. But the paras kept tripping and falling in the pitch blackness; in the end, the officers had no option but the dangerous one of using torches. When they had taken

Above: An Israeli command unit returns a sniper's fire from behind a wall. Moving through the built-up areas was a nightmare, as hostile fire might erupt from any direction at any moment.

Below: Within the cramped confines of the Old City, shrapnel from Jordanian shellfire and mortar bombs exacted a high toll among the Israeli assault force. Heavy casualties caused by Jordanian support weapons placed the paratroopers' first-aid facilities under great strain.

the school, A Company moved on towards the Ambassador Hotel, together with D Company; B and C Companies moved towards Ammunition Hill.

As dawn broke (at about 0340 hours) the paras were engaged in a deadly, exhausting fight for the hill. In the trenches and bunkers it was often very difficult to tell friend from foe, and the fighting was further confused by Jordanian sniping from hills to the north. Tanks came up in support, but close-quarters fighting against prepared positions is a tanker's nightmare, and they needed infantry protection against bazookas and recoilless rifles. Soon, the paras had emptied the spare loaded magazines they had brought with them, and had to refill magazines by hand from ammunition boxes – a tiring, fiddly task when under fire. But gradually, the hill was cleared, and the final, so-called 'great bunker' was taken at 0515.

Meanwhile, the 71st Battalion was also meeting stiff resistance in its attack. Having had the most problems in assembling for the assault, this battalion also had difficulty in finding its way once it was into the Jordanian lines. The difficulty of finding the right road in the darkness with only photographs to guide them was magnified by the need to clear hidden Jordanian positions. Dropping grenades into emplacements, and carefully moving along the sheltered sides of streets, the Israelis began clearing the area between the frontier and the Nablus Road, and had a stroke of luck when the Jordanian defenders of the street leading to Wadi El-Joz were taken by surprise. A company of paras moved rapidly down the street to set up positions at this important intersection.

Although the advance was generally going well, the Jordanian support weapons soon picked out the assembly area of the Israelis, and the brigade's mortar crews and recoilless rifle operators suffered casualties as artillery fire began to zero in on them. The breaches in the front-line defences were soon being crossed by the wounded returning from the fight up ahead, some stoical but others screaming with pain. The medical resources of the brigade were becoming dangerously stretched by the mounting casualties in the attacking battalions and among the support units that were under artillery and machine-gun fire.

One heavy machine gun in particular had caused great concern

One heavy machine gun in particular had caused great concern as it swept the breaches with fire before it was knocked out by a bazooka; and in spite of many efforts, a light machine gun proved endlessly troublesome. It would stop as soon as a shell burst near it, then open up again. A group of staff officers from the 28th Battalion volunteered to finish it off; but when they tried to approach it they were caught in a trap, and the commander of the support company, leading the attempt, was seriously wounded.

With bullets flying and shells bursting around them, the

Above: A paratrooper cautiously peers round the corner of a building. He is armed with a Uzi sub-machine gun.
Left: A paratrooper of the 55th Parachute Brigade at the Battle of Jerusalem in 1967. The men of the 55th Brigade wore camouflage fatigues from France with an olive-green combat jacket worn on top. This man's helmet is the British paratroop model, and he is armed with the 7.62mm FN-FAL rifle from Belgium.

43

men of the 28th Battalion moved off to begin their part of the assault soon after the 71st Battalion had gone through the breach in the wire. One shell chanced to injure the deputy commander of D Company, while there were serious officer casualties when a Jordanian 25pdr struck battalion headquarters. After a seemingly interminable wait, it was dawn before the first members of the 28th Battalion had got to the Jordanian side of the wire, and then they had to fight their way south.

Fighting in the daylight proved, in some ways, worse than the night fighting. Now, snipers could fire without the flash of their muzzles giving away their position, and Jordanian artillery observers had a better view of events. Some of the districts through which the men of the 28th were moving were supposed to have been cleared, but the Israelis soon found that enemy troops could easily infiltrate back into good positions. The building of the Moslem Council had to be cleared three times to make certain that a single shot, or a carefully lobbed grenade, would not take its toll of the advancing Israelis.

The squad pulled out and a tank put two shells into the upper stories

The task of moving down Saladin Street was given to C Company but, unable to identify the area properly, it went down Nablus Road. Here the paras had to flush out the YMCA building, from which there was considerable fire. Entering it cautiously, they found most of it empty, finding only the base of a machine-gun mounting. Suddenly the squad that was investigating the situation was fired upon, and men went down wounded. Time was too short to waste on just one obstacle, and a hand-to-hand combat would have resulted in further casualties. The squad pulled out, and a supporting tank put two shells into the upper stories; the advance went on.

About 0500, there was a lull and the men of the 28th Battalion were ordered to halt. This was a nerve-racking moment, because the risk of a sniper's bullet, or of a well-aimed salvo of artillery shells, was as great as ever. Then the advance began again with more tank support. The main task now was to get to the Rockefeller Museum, an imposing new building that dominated the approaches to the northeast corner of the Old City. The roar of the tank guns when they fired almost deafened the paratroopers as the sound echoed between the high buildings. The paras also found it difficult to communicate with the tank crews because the cables for the external telephones had been cut by shrapnel, or were turned off so that the tankers could listen to the stream of orders they were getting on their radio net.

By 0800, the 55th Brigade had performed brilliantly. All its objectives were secured, and it had set the scene for further advance. From Ammunition Hill in the north through Sheikh Jarrah, the Ambassador Hotel, and down to Wadi El-Joz, a line had been established that gave contact with the slopes

THE JORDAN ARAB ARMY

When the Jordan Arab Army crossed the Israeli border in 1967, many of the troops would have recalled the attack on Jerusalem made by their predecessors, the Arab Legion of Transjordan, nearly 20 years before. After the 1948 Arab-Israeli War parts of Palestine were placed under Jordanian authority, and the combined population of the West Bank and Transjordan totalled about three million.

Following the war, the Arab Legion had been increased to 10,000 men in anticipation of further war with Israel. Originally a force recruited almost exclusively from Bedouin tribes, the Arab Legion received a substantial influx of educated Palestinians after 1948. However, after an attempted coup in 1956 King Hussein made radical changes to secure a more loyal army. He dismissed all his British officers and renamed the force the Jordan Arab Army. Rigorous political screening of recruits was introduced and the number of Palestinians in service was reduced.

By the time of the Six-Day War of 1967, the Army had grown into a highly efficient combat force of 50,000 men.

Far left, top: Troops of the Jordan Arab Army wait impatiently to enter the Old City.
Far left: An Israeli paratrooper, wounded during the fighting in the Old City, receives first aid from his comrades.

Fight for the Holy City

Below: Two Israelis, worn out by hours of hard fighting, pause to grab a hasty meal.

of Mount Scopus and promised imminent relief for the besieged garrison; while in the south, the capture of the Rockefeller Museum made an assault against the Old City a practical possibility. Indeed, paras of the 28th Battalion had

set themselves up in the Rivoli Hotel opposite Herod's Gate, and when they were not engaging the defenders of the walls of the Old City they were able to sample the delights of the hotel's kitchens, and have a bath.

The casualties sustained by the brigade in reaching these objectives had been horrific – but the achievement had been immense. Gur visited the troops at the Rockefeller Museum. Although many had no previous experience of real action, he noted that already they were comporting themselves like veterans; they knew exactly where enemy fire might come from, and where to find precisely the safest places to relax.

Left: Israeli paratroops carrying out a sweep in the Old City climb the Temple Mount, towards the Dome of the Rock, the third holiest mosque in the world. Above: General Uzi Narkiss (centre), walks through the Old City towards the Western (Wailing) Wall after the defeat of the Jordanians.

Above: Israeli paratroopers at the Wailing Wall on 7 June 1967. There was a brief ceremony to commemorate success, and then the paras returned to the fighting.

The ranks of the three battalions were thinned by the pounding they had taken during the assault, but there was no shortage of volunteers to replace the dead and wounded. The mortar crews and anti-tank personnel were now anxious to get into the front line – especially as the Old City was beckoning. Morale was sky-high, and Gur prepared to move the 66th Battalion further south to participate in another day's fighting.

Narkiss, desperate to finish things off and to get into the Holy City, ordered Gur to concentrate on taking the last Jordanian strongpoint in the region, the Augusta Victoria Hospital on a ridge to the south of Mount Scopus, and then to prepare an encirclement of the Old City. The plans for the assault were swiftly drawn up, and it was decided to wait until after 1930 hours, when darkness fell, before going into the attack.

The assault on the Augusta Victoria Hospital got off to a bad start, when some troops strayed too close to the walls of the Old City and were fired on from there; and then, at 2140, Gur was informed that 40 Patton tanks of the Jordanian Army had been seen on the reverse side of the slope his men were to attack. With only four Shermans as support, Gur could not risk the assault. He decided to wait until the next day, when aerial support could be called in. Anti-tank dispositions were made and then the soldiers tried to snatch a little sleep.

Gur's new plan was to attack at about 1130 hours on 7 June, by which time the Israeli Air Force should have dispersed the Pattons. The Israeli high command decided, however, that the attack should go in much earlier in the morning, at 0830. Again, there was frantic haste to reschedule operations, for the new attack was to be mounted from Mount Scopus as well as from across the Kidron valley.

Had the Israelis known it, such frenzied preparations were hardly necessary. Far from being able to bring up substantial armoured reinforcements, Brigadier Ata Ali had been completely cut off by the success of Israeli moves to north and south, and by the Israeli Air Force's devastating attacks on road convoys. His troops began a skilful withdrawal in the early hours of 7 June.

At 0804, just before his attacks were to start, Gur was at last given the order that he was so anxious to receive: he was told to take the Old City. Immediately after the air attacks on the Augusta Victoria Ridge, his men stormed over it, and at 0930 he was able to give the historic order to his brigade that the time for waiting was past.

The entry into the Old City was to be via the Lion's Gate, which was the only one able to take tanks, and as the armoured support of the paratroopers approached this point of entry, there was some sporadic defensive fire. Gur himself led the entry into the Old City, and his troops met only light resistance from isolated snipers. At about 1000, he reached the Wailing Wall. The brigade's ordnance officer produced a bottle of whisky, and passed it round. The 55th Brigade had won a victory that no one in Israel would ever forget – a victory of religious as well as political significance.

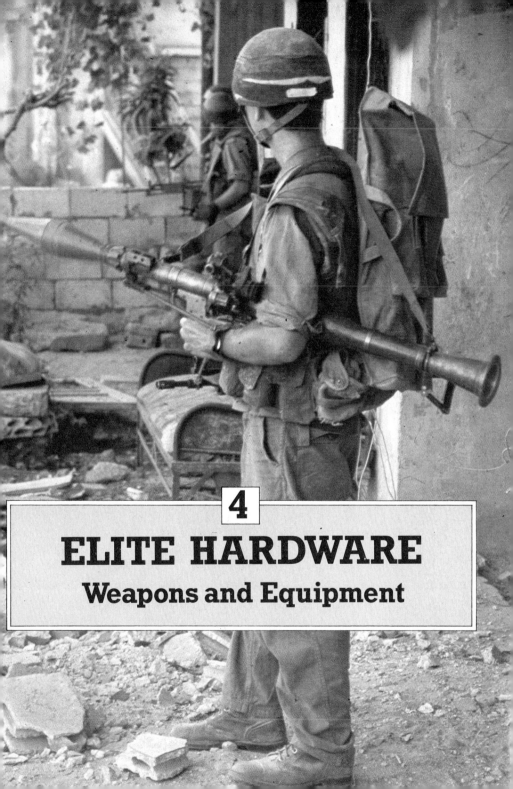

4

ELITE HARDWARE
Weapons and Equipment

Previous page: Armed with an RPG-7, an Israeli paratrooper stands beside a ruined building in Beirut.
Below: The Israeli version of the British 2in mortar, built by Israeli Military Industries.
Below right: Men of Haganah practise with a homemade mortar. The experience gained during the struggle for independence was put to good use in building up an indigenous Israeli arms industry.

THE BRITISH 6th Airborne Division was stationed in Palestine in the late 1940s, and when the Israeli Army formed its first parachute units their operational techniques were based on British practice. Many Jews had served in the British Army, and large numbers of British weapons remained in Palestine after 1948. As a result the Israeli troopers carried Sten guns and Lee-Enfield rifles, with 2in mortars and Bren light machine guns for their immediate support and 3in mortars and 6pdr anti-tank guns drawn by jeeps as their heavy support.

The War of Independence of 1948–49, when Israel was fighting for its very existence, taught the lesson that the first weapon priority was a reliable sub-machine gun, and so the Uzi 9mm weapon was produced. Built first with a wooden stock, a folding-stock version rapidly followed, and this was

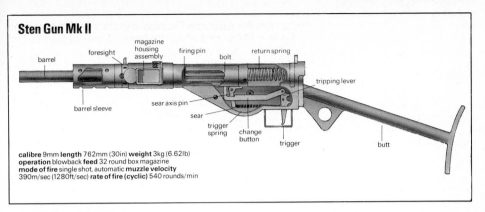

Sten Gun Mk II

barrel — foresight — magazine housing assembly — firing pin — bolt — return spring — tripping lever — barrel sleeve — sear axis pin — sear — trigger spring — change button — trigger — butt

calibre 9mm **length** 762mm (30in) **weight** 3kg (6.62lb)
operation blowback **feed** 32 round box magazine
mode of fire single shot, automatic **muzzle velocity**
390m/sec (1280ft/sec) **rate of fire (cyclic)** 540 rounds/min

Left: Israeli troops armed with Stens and Czech 7.92mm VZ 24 rifles man a trench during the 1956 Sinai campaign.

Uzi sub-machine gun

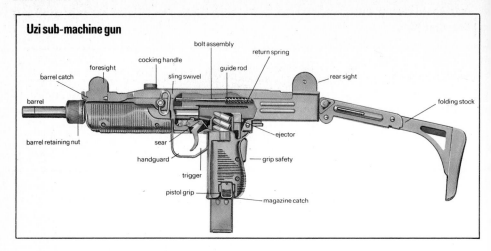

The heterogeneous mass of weaponry used by Israeli troops during their fight for independence in 1948-49 made the maintenance of weapons and the supply of ammunition difficult. After the 1949 armistices the Israeli Defence Forces (IDF) emphasised the need for good standardised smallarms, and Major Uziel Gal began to work on a sub-machine gun design that would fulfil this requirement. In 1952 the IDF brought this weapon, the Uzi, into service.

The Uzi was based on the design of the Czech CZ-23 sub-machine gun and the two are visibly similar. When closed, the bolt wraps around the barrel and this enables the receiver (the part of the weapon containing the bolt assembly) to be kept short. The compact size of the Uzi makes it a very handy weapon and the presence of the magazine in the pistol grip reduces the possibility of fumbles when reloading. The stock is either wooden or folding metal and there are 32 rounds in the standard magazine.

immediately adopted by the paratroopers in place of their aging Sten guns. The Uzi was light, reliable and effective, and served the Israelis well through a succession of bitter wars of survival. The Lee-Enfield gave way to the 7.92mm Mauser rifle, and in an effort to find a machine gun of compatible calibre the Israelis adopted the American Johnson design of 1944, calling it the 'Dror'.

The Johnson was an unusual weapon in many ways. In the first place it operated by recoil, one of the few light machine guns to use this system. On firing, the barrel recoils, locked to the bolt, for a short distance and then stops; the bolt unlocks and continues rearward, then drives forward again to strip a round from the magazine and fire it. The magazine was inserted on the left side of the gun, and it was possible to 'top up' a partly emptied magazine through a door in the right side of the weapon, using either loose rounds or clips of five cartridges. Another innovation was that when firing single shots, the bolt closed and locked and the trigger was then pressed to fire, but when firing at automatic the bolt remained open when the trigger was released, only running forward to load and fire when the trigger was pressed. In this way the barrel remained empty during pauses in automatic fire and allowed air to pass through and cool it. The barrel could be rapidly removed and the whole weapon could then be packed into a compact space, an ideal configuration for airborne use.

Johnson, a captain in the US Marines, had first put this weapon forward to the US forces in 1941 but they were intent upon a belt-fed weapon and after long trials turned it down; he made some minor improvements in 1944 but his design was still magazine-fed and fared little better. The sale of the design to Israel was his only commercial success with the gun, but in service it proved a disappointment. The system of operation was sound, and the weapon was well made, but the drawback was the movement of the recoiling barrel, which had to pass through bushings in the outer barrel jacket. This

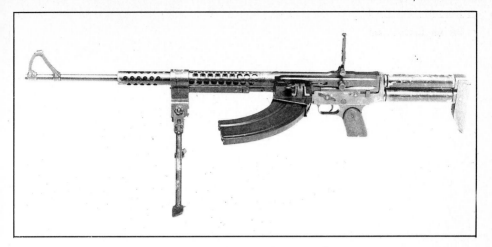

constant movement, allied to the abrasive dust of the Middle Eastern terrain, soon wore away the faces of barrel and bush so that the barrel became loose and accuracy vanished. The Dror was removed from service after only a few years' use.

In the late 1950s it was decided to standardise the Nato 7.62mm cartridge in Israeli service, and the FN-FAL semi-automatic rifle was adopted as the general service weapon for all forces. To accompany this in the light machine gun slot, the heavy-barrelled (HB) version of the FAL was adopted. This, as its name implies, was no more than a standard rifle mechanism with a heavy, fixed, barrel and a bipod. Versions of both the rifle and the HB rifle with folding metal butts were adopted for use by the paratroops.

The support and heavy weapons also underwent revision in the late 1950s. The British 2in mortar was now being

Above: The Dror, an Israeli modification of the US Johnson light machine gun. Although the weapon was a good design, the firing action was not suitable to dusty, Middle Eastern conditions.

Below: Israeli paratroopers, armed with Uzis and a heavy-barrelled FN during the raid on the Jordanian town of Samu in 1966. Both these weapons have now been officially replaced by the Galil.

manufactured in Israel as the 52mm IMI mortar, and this continued in service since it was light and effective. The 6pdr anti-tank gun could no longer be relied on to damage modern tanks, and ammunition was no longer available from Britain or any other supplier, so it was dropped and replaced by the American 106mm recoilless (RCL) rifle. For lighter anti-tank defence, required by the paratroops during the early stages of an assault before heavy weapons could be brought in, the Swedish 84mm Carl Gustav recoilless gun was adopted. The Finnish company Tampella, experts in mortar design, were approached for a new 81mm model,

Left:: A US-supplied 106mm recoilless gun in use with Israeli forces on the Golan Heights in 1967. The paratroopers use this weapon to provide heavy anti-tank defence.

and this was eventually produced in Israel by the Soltam company.

The 106mm RCL rifle M40 is, in fact, of 105mm calibre; its name was deliberately chosen in order to distinguish it from an earlier 105mm model which was unsuccessful. Like all RCL guns it relies upon ejecting a proportion of the propellant gas to the rear to counterbalance the recoil, and, although rifled, it fires a fin-stabilised shaped-charge anti-tank shell which is very effective against modern tanks,

though no longer capable of penetrating frontal armour of the heaviest types. Firing in the anti-tank role it has an effective range of about 1200m, but it is also provided with an anti-personnel shell of conventional spin-stabilised type which has a maximum range in excess of 7000m. The gun is fitted with a .50in calibre spotting rifle on top of the barrel; this fires a special explosive bullet which produces a vivid flash and puff of smoke on impact and which is ballistically matched to the anti-tank projectile. The gunner takes aim and fires the spotting rifle until he obtains a hit on the target, then fires the main gun, the shell following the same trajectory and striking in the same place as the spotting rifle bullet.

The 84mm Carl Gustav is a much smaller weapon which can be fired from a man's shoulder. It fires a shaped-charge

Below: An Israeli paratrooper during jump training. He is wearing a French parachute, based on the design of the US T-7.
Below right: The versatility of the Galil is indicated by the wide range of attachments provided.

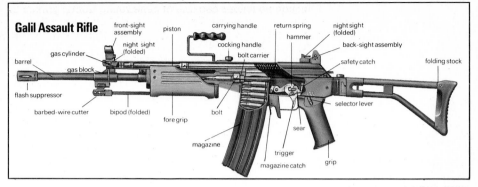

Galil Assault Rifle — front-sight assembly, piston, carrying handle, return spring, night sight (folded), gas cylinder, night sight (folded), cocking handle, hammer, back-sight assembly, barrel, gas block, bolt carrier, safety catch, folding stock, flash suppressor, barbed-wire cutter, bipod (folded), fore grip, bolt, selector lever, magazine, sear, trigger, grip, magazine catch

During the Six-Day War the Israeli Army's primary smallarm was the FN-FAL rifle. It proved to be prone to jamming in desert conditions and after the war the Israeli Defence Forces tested a number of designs for a possible replacement for the FAL. The standard they were measured against was the AK-47 and, perhaps not surprisingly, an Israeli design based on the AK-47 – the Galil – proved to be the best. The Galil uses the 5.56 × 45mm cartridge, like the US M16.

Although the design uses a number of Stoner system parts (Eugene Stoner designed a number of important smallarms, including the M16) the system of operation is a gas action similar to the AK-47, The Galil has a flash suppressor on the muzzle and the stock can be either wood, plastic or metal folding. A bipod may be supplied to enable the Galil to be used as a squad support weapon. Three sizes of magazine box are provided: for 12, 35 (the most common) and 50 rounds.

shell which is drag-stabilised in flight and has a maximum effective range of about 500m. It can also fire anti-personnel high explosive, smoke and illuminating shells, making it an extremely versatile support weapon. It weighs just over 14kg and thus can be carried by one man during a parachute descent, giving the force an immediate anti-armour capability which is effective against all but the heaviest tanks.

By the end of the 1960s the Israeli airborne forces had amassed a useful volume of combat experience and they began to re-assess their weapon requirements. The most basic need was to integrate the personal weapons, both to simplify ammunition provision and to provide each soldier with one weapon which could function as a close-in personal defence or as a longer-range offensive armament. Early in 1972 the Galil rifle was adopted to replace the FN-FAL and the Uzi sub-machine gun as the para's personal weapon.

The Galil was a 5.56mm calibre automatic rifle, the design of which leaned heavily on the Soviet Kalashnikov AK-47 for its basic mechanical principles; Israeli experience of the Kalashnikov in Arab hands had shown its reliability in harsh conditions. The Galil was gas-operated, with a rotating bolt, and fed from a 30-round magazine. Fitted with a bipod and a

50-round magazine, it also functioned as the squad automatic. Since it had a folding stock, it was compact for carriage and air-dropping, and its automatic fire capability and short overall length made it a good substitute for a sub-machine gun. Thus one weapon replaced two, although, as is often the case, the replacement did neither job quite as successfully as the two weapons it superseded. The Uzi, with its 9mm Parabellum bullet, had perhaps a better knock-down power at short ranges, while the FN-FAL in 7.62mm calibre had a longer effective range and a heavier bullet. But consideration of the combat role of the Israeli airborne force suggests that neither of these two drawbacks was really vital and certainly not sufficient to prevent the adoption of the Galili across the board.

Another weapon which had confronted the Israelis in their wars against the Arabs had been the Soviet RPG-7 anti-tank rocket launcher. This shoulder-fired lightweight weapon has a formidable punch against armour and there are few

Below: Israeli M113 armoured personnel carriers and M3 half-tracks meet on the Golan Heights. These are the basic transport for Israeli paras operating as mechanised infantry – a role they have frequently been called on to play in Israel's long series of wars.

Western equivalents which have the same favourable combination of weight, range and power. As a result of their several offensive actions against different Arab states, the Israelis amassed a considerable quantity of these weapons and most of them appear to have been earmarked for use by airborne forces, generally replacing the Carl Gustav RCL rifle. The weapon itself is little more than a tube with a sight, and weighs half as much as the Carl Gustav. The rockets weigh slightly less than a round of 84mm ammunition, but while there is an anti-personnel rocket, there is no smoke or illuminating warhead available. Nevertheless the anti-armour performance is what counts, and with the capability of penetrating 320mm of armour plate at a maximum effective range of 500m, the RPG-7 is an extremely useful addition to the airborne armoury.

In order to augment the RPG-7 and to replace the aging 52mm mortar, the Israelis have adopted a range of rifle grenades. The muzzle of the Galil rifle is shaped with

THE MAKING OF A PARA

The men of Israel's regular paratroop brigade have always maintained high standards of fighting ability. To maintain the formation's excellent record, new recruits are put through an exhaustive training programme that pushes them to the limits of their endurance.

After induction, each volunteer is sent on a basic course that is designed to build up his fitness and develop his combat skills. Particular emphasis is placed on nightfighting techniques. Those who pass this first stage are then sent on a parachuting course.

After this phase, the new paratrooper embarks on a course devised to improve his knowledge of combined operations. Joint manoeuvres with tank and artillery units are organised, and each recruit is taught how to work with helicopters, assault craft and armoured personnel carriers. The next stage of training is the squad commander course, in which the recruit learns the vital skills of a junior NCO. All paratroopers attend this programme and are then assigned different roles. Each man is taught a specialised skill (these skills include communications, demolition techniques and medical procedures). A percentage of recruit is selected to attend Officer School, where they are groomed for higher command.

22m-diameter bearing rings, so that there is no need to fit an auxiliary grenade launcher to the rifle. The grenades are fin-stabilised and have a hollow tail boom carrying the fins, ahead of which is the warhead. The hollow tail slips snugly over the rifle muzzle, and the trooper loads a special blank cartridge which is supplied with the grenade. He clips to the grenade tail a disposable plastic sight, takes aim, and fires the rifle. The gas generated by the special cartridge propels the grenade from the muzzle, the sight falls off, and the rifle is immediately ready for another grenade or for normal use.

Three basic grenades are issued to airborne forces. The AP-30 is a general-purpose anti-personnel grenade which is, as a bonus, capable of penetrating up to 8mm of steel, so that it can be used against vehicles; it has a maximum range of 300m. The AP-65 is heavier, another dual-purpose design, capable of piercing 13mm of steel, and has a maximum range of 250m. The AT-52 is purely an anti-armour grenade, using a shaped-charge warhead, and will penetrate 150mm of

Below: Israeli paratroopers in Beirut. They are armed with a variety of weapons. In the centre is a grenadier armed with an M16 with M203 40mm grenade launcher attached.

دائرة الجوازات والسفر والجنسية
PASSPORT TRAVELL
AND NATIONALITY DEPT

Right: Israeli troops rest after heavy fighting at Rafah Junction in 1967. They are armed with heavy-barrelled FNs for squad support, Uzis and a World War II German FG 42 paratroop rifle.

armour or even greater thickness of concrete, making it effective against light field defences.

The replacement of the 52mm mortar with the rifle grenade was a partial success; it made the distribution of ammunition rather easier, and it gave individuals the ability to project fire to about 300m without having to call for the mortar. But the 52mm had ranged to 450m, and this additional 150m of range was sorely missed in some situations. The Soltam company, however, produced a weapon which was not only to replace the 52mm model (which was, after all, a design from the 1930s) but was to give the airborne section even greater power and range.

The whole Israeli Army is looking for a weapon to deal with modern Soviet tanks

Soltam already manufactured a conventional 60mm mortar which had been adopted by the Israeli Army as a standard infantry platoon weapon; this was of the usual form, a barrel resting on a heavy baseplate and mounted on an adjustable bipod. It fired a 1.75kg bomb to a range of 2550m, but it was a heavy weapon, weighing 16.5kg ready to fire. The company now produced a 'Commando' version of the mortar which was simply a short barrel with a small baseplate, a handgrip and a rudimentary elevation level. The soldier merely gripped the handle, placed the baseplate on the ground, looked along a line painted on the barrel to give him direction and tilted the barrel until the level on the side indicated that it was correctly angled for the desired range. He then dropped a bomb into it and pulled the trigger in the breech end of the tube to send the bomb off to a maximum range of 900m.

It would be a bold prophet who attempted to foresee the Israelis' next move; but one obvious area which requires attention is the anti-armour field. While the weapons described above are good, they are simply not good enough in view of the enormous number of modern Soviet tanks which Israel's potential enemies can muster, and the whole Israeli Army, not only the airborne forces, is looking for a portable anti-tank weapon capable of dealing with these tanks. A great deal of work went into a missile project called 'Picket', which had several advanced features including a gyroscopically stabilised flight line which made aiming much easier. But this appears to have failed, and has been abandoned. Presently much developmental work is being put into the 'B-300' system, a shoulder-fired semi-disposable weapon which launches a powerful rocket to a range of 400m. The warhead is said to be capable of penetrating armour in excess of 400mm thickness at an impact angle of 65°, which suggests that it will defeat the frontal armour of any existing tank. The weapon, with three rockets, weighs 16kg and separates to form a package less than 750mm long. With a weapon of this nature, airborne forces would be secure against armoured attack at the landing zone in the vulnerable period before their heavy weapons can be brought up.

Above: A squad of Israeli troops waits to go into action in Lebanon, 1982. They are armed with the standard paratroop weapons – Galils and an RPG-7 for anti-tank work.

5
THE YOM KIPPUR WAR
The Paras Battle for Suez

Previous page: Israeli troops on captured OT-62 APCs enter Suez town, Surprised by the intensity of the Egyptian resistance, the Israeli paras had to dig into their reserves of courage to hold out.
Below: Israeli armour escorts bridgelaying equipment to the Suez Canal. The crossing of the Canal made the Egyptian forces on the east bank dangerously vulnerable.

ON 25 OCTOBER 1973 an Israeli armoured brigade led by Colonel Arich Keren rolled into the Egyptian-held town of Suez in what was to have been an easy mopping-up operation towards the end of the Yom Kippur War. Behind them was a force of paratroops – about 100 of Israel's finest fighting men who had earlier achieved the crossing of the Suez Canal – commanded by Lieutenant-Colonel 'Yossi', As the tanks entered the town, however, heavy fire rained down upon them from all sides, and 20 out of the 24 tank commanders (who had been standing in their open turrets) were wounded within minutes.

The leading element of the para battalion also came under fire in their eight captured half-tracks, a jeep and a bus. Leaping from their vehicles, the paras ran to clear out the nearest buildings, but the fire intensified and the unit was split up. The company commander, 'Buki', was killed along with several of his men as he led two platoons to the safety of a house, and the rest of the company followed the half-track of the battalion commander to the shelter of the police station

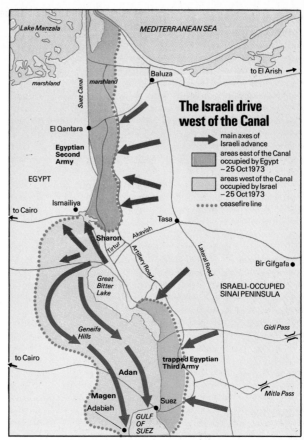

The Israeli drive west of the Canal

→ main axes of Israeli advance

▨ areas east of the Canal occupied by Egypt – 25 Oct 1973

▨ areas west of the Canal occupied by Israel – 25 Oct 1973

••••• ceasefire line

near by. Unfortunately the lead half-track was hit by an anti-tank shell, killing the communications officer, operations sergeant, battalion medical orderly and radio operator and wounding the commander and the operations officer as well as two other soldiers. The driver of another half-track, Michael Shor, was shot in the head but continued to drive his crew to safety until a second bullet to the head killed him.

The battalion second-in-command who was bringing up the rear managed to turn his half-track round and escape from the town after a fierce firefight with dozens of Egyptians. The HQ platoon commander in another vehicle at the rear of the column dropped off his men to evacuate wounded tank crew. When he returned to the town, there was no sign of his men – they were later found among the dead.

The situation inside the police station was chaotic, as a number of Egyptian policemen attempted to resist the paras. Some were shot as the paras took over the building, and some were captured and thrown out into the street, where they were shot by their own side. The intelligence officer, 'Tzachi' took some men outside to cover stray paras who

On 6 October 1973, the Jewish religious festival known as Yom Kippur, Israel was simultaneously attacked by Egyptian forces across the Suez Canal and by Syrian forces on the Golan Heights. Egypt had been carefully preparing for this assault for some time, and its troops succeeded in getting across the heavily fortified Canal and striking into the Sinai Desert. The Syrians were not so fortunate and made little headway in the north, losing around 1400 tanks to the Israelis' 250. Having cemented its defences on the Golan Heights, the IDF turned to the Sinai front and succeeded in pushing the Egyptians back over the Canal. A ceasefire came into force on 22 October, but sporadic fighting continued until the 28th.

were still arriving, and succeeded in defending the building from an Egyptian counterattack. One very welcome arrival was the battalion doctor and medical team, who fought their way from house to house to the police station, and managed to get inside with the medical supplies. They immediately set to work tending the many wounded paras lined up in the corridor, and continued to do so – working with one hand and firing with the other – when attacked by a group of Egyptians who had been overlooked when the building was cleared.

The Egyptians had surrounded the house, placing mines in the road

The situation was even more desperate in the other building, where the remnants of Buki's two platoons were holed out. There were 18 men in one apartment (three of whom were wounded), four in another apartment in the same building, and a further eight in hiding. None of these groups was aware of each other's existence nor that the remainder of the battalion was only 20–30m away, in the comparative safety of the police station. The Egyptians had surrounded the house, placing mines in the road to prevent reinforcements being brought up, and made several unsuccessful assaults. The group of 18 men, who had left their spare ammunition and supplies in their vehicles, pinned their hopes on a night-time escape bid, using the half-track that was sitting right outside, its engine still running – but halfway through the afternoon the motor died, and their last hope with it.

At the police station First Lieutenant David Amit was promoted from platoon commander to senior officer, as all the other officers had been killed or wounded. Towards the end of the first day, each soldier was down to one ammunition

Far right top: Israeli troops cross the Suez Canal and move out to take on Egyptian forces.
Right: Suez town under Israeli bombardment. Artillery support was an important factor in the eventual safe withdrawal of the trapped paras.
Far right: Part of the arsenal that the Israelis deployed against Suez town – captured Soviet-made 'Katyusha' rocket launchers, here sending off a salvo.

APPROACH TO SUEZ

By 22 October the IDF was hitting back at the Egyptian Third Army that was occupying Suez and a small area of Sinai east of the Canal. The Israeli forces, under Major-General Avraham Adan, had cut off the Egyptians' supply lines based on the Cairo–Suez highway and the Third Army was surrounded. The position was best summed up by the Egyptian commander, General Wassil: 'The Cairo–Suez road is completely blocked. I'm trapped inside…the army is cut off, no longer under Arab control.' Although cornered, the Egyptians were not yet beaten, as the Israeli paras were to find out to their cost when they motored into Suez on 25 October.

The attack on Suez town was a tactical blunder, which could easily have been avoided. Nothing was to be gained by entering the town and there was a lack of basic intelligence as to the situation there. The troops taking part were expecting an easy mopping-up operation, which accounted for the heavy casualties they sustained. When Major-General Avraham Adan asked permission to attack, the answer was: 'If it's going to be another Beersheba, go ahead, but if it's going to be a Stalingrad, no!' (Beersheba fell surprisingly easily to Israeli forces in the 1948 War.)

magazine and one grenade. There were only two water-bottles and these were saved for the wounded.

Back at HQ, the commanders began to see the enormous folly of the attack on Suez. The paras were cut off and separated into several small groups – nobody knew how many, or how many in each – and each group was surrounded by well-equipped, numerically superior Arab forces. Artillery or air support was out of the question – no one knew the positions of the various groups. A relieving infantry force was sent in that night, but despite shouts and flares fired by the 18 soldiers in the house, they did not locate them and withdrew. Several photo-reconnaissance aircraft flew over the town at first light the next day, but succeeded only in spotting the four-man group in the house. Finally, the brigade commander, who was still outside the town, got through to Amit on the radio and ordered him to break out, with all his men, under cover of darkness. Amit flatly refused to obey the order on the grounds that it would mean leaving the wounded behind. 'Either we all come out, or none of us comes out,' he replied.

An attempt at dawn to reach the abandoned half-tracks

Right: The paraphernalia of close-quarters combat in urban areas – festooned with ammunition belts, this paratrooper is moving forward to find another position from which to give covering fire to his comrades.
Far right: An Israeli gives covering fire during an advance in a built-up area.

had been successful, and some ammunition and a few jerrycans of water had been carried back to the besieged force in the police station. The wounded had been taken down to a basement, but the battalion commander, Yossi, refused to go. He was slipping in and out of a coma, but when he was conscious he would crawl among his men giving them encouragement. Morale was also boosted by the information that the four paras spotted by the reconnaissance plane were still alive and holed up in a building only a few metres away from the police station.

Amit began planning to bring the four into the police station, under cover of darkness. Using their radios, Amit and the commander of the four, First Lieutenant Gil, agreed that the incoming troops would give a series of short flashes with their torches in order to let the men in the police station know that they were on their way and to identify their position. Amit was to signal back, giving Gil the direction of the entrance to the police building. Amit's men were to give covering fire if the manoeuvre was discovered by the Egyptians.

Gil and his men began a slow, wary movement out of the apartment. Suddenly, they heard the sound of men in a nearby apartment, Inexplicably, perhaps miraculously, no one fired. The sounds came from the 18 paras who, unknown to Gil, had been almost next door. Their mutual surprise and joy at meeting each other received an added boost when suddenly, attracted by the sound of Hebrew being spoken, another eight soldiers came out of hiding. This

Above: The end of the fighting in Suez. Israeli troops maintain a careful watch as UN troops in blue helmets police the ceasefire line.

69

Above: Grim and tense, Israelis prepare to go into action against Egyptian forces. The Yom Kippur War had been a long, hard struggle, and the sudden difficulties of the fighting in Suez town were the last thing that the men of the IDF wanted.

combined force, now 30 strong, made its way towards Amit's flashlight and reached the safety of the police building. In the station, the atmosphere was almost festive. It immediately became obvious why the soldiers in the apartment block did not know that the major part of the force was only a few metres away, despite the noise of the shooting – there were no windows that faced the police station.

The force in the police station now numbered 80 men and their situation had been altered sufficiently for them to try a breakout. Amit reported to HQ that they would make the attempt that night. The plan was to leave the building and to regroup in the courtyard outside. However, the lookouts inside the building reported seeing a large Egyptian force outside and on the neighbouring roofs. The paratroopers, who had neither eaten nor slept for two days, were now unwilling to give up the 'safety' of the building, and morale sank again so low that Amit decided to postpone the attempt.

All the paras were now together in one place and ready to go

Only at 0200 did Amit decide that the time was right to move. He radioed brigade command to give them the news they had been waiting for. All the paras were now together in one place and ready to go. Israeli artillery units had been given the exact coordinates of the police station and the route out of Suez. They were to provide cover for the retreat.

The wounded refused to be carried on stretchers, in order not to slow the force down. Yossi walked all the way, moaning in agony with every step he took. As they retreated, the Israelis could hear the Egyptian soldiers calling to each other as they passed the houses where they were posted. The paras had been ordered not to open fire unless fired upon, so as not to give themselves away. Amazingly, the 80 men withdrew without having a shot fired at them. Either the Egyptians were too concerned with the nearby shelling, or they mistook the large force for a unit of Egyptians, or perhaps they simply did not notice.

It was two hours before the Israelis reached the water channel on the outskirts of the town of Suez. Egyptian troops in the area had spotted them, but decided not to engage such a large force. Everyone was aware that if they could make the crossing, they would be out of the area controlled by the Egyptians and back into friendly territory. They turned west along the channel, heading for a distant bridge. Almost immediately they came upon a bridge that was not marked on their maps. After checking it for mines and booby traps, 80 tired and hungry Israeli paratroops crossed the bridge to safety. A unit of an armoured division was waiting, and the tank searchlights were turned on to direct the paras home.

The men who had gone into Suez for what was to have been a simple mopping-up operation, walked out of the town at 0430, two days after riding in on their half-tracks. Eighty Israeli soldiers died in the fighting.

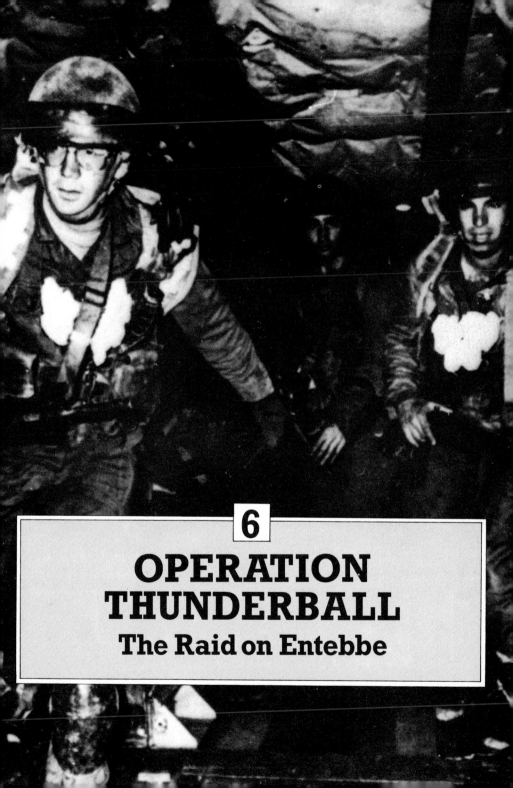

6

OPERATION THUNDERBALL
The Raid on Entebbe

In the immediate aftermath of the hijacking of Air France Flight 139 on 27 June 1976, the government of Israel had to find as much information as it could before an effective response could be formulated. The first break came on 30 June, when a batch of non-Jewish hostages was released. Arriving at Orly airport in Paris, the freed passengers were interviewed by Israeli intelligence. The numbers of terrorists, their weapons, and their relationship with the Ugandan government were subjects of particular interest.

A high-ranking team of military and civilian experts considered the options open to the Israelis. Three military solutions were considered: a paradrop onto Lake Victoria followed by a water-borne assault; a direct attack from Kenya; and the airborne landing at Entebbe. The last-named was considered the most feasible, but before it could be put into action more details were needed. An Israeli firm had constructed several buildings at Entebbe and their blueprints were of great value; all information that could be obtained from international airlines was collated, as was everything that could be found out about the Ugandan armed forces.

The final decision to go for Entebbe was not taken until 3 July – but by then a formidable dossier on the target had been built up.

Previous page: Israeli paras prepare to go into action.
Far right, top: Mordechai Gur, Israeli Chief of Staff at the time of the hijack.
Far right: Major-General Dan Shomron, who planned the raid with Gur, and led it personally.

SHORTLY BEFORE dawn on 3 July 1976, specialist paratroop units of the Israeli Defence Forces (IDF) loaded their equipment and drove to a nearby airbase, where ground-crews stood ready to lash their vehicles into the bellies of four Hercules transports. Elsewhere on the field, the crew of a Boeing 707, fitted out as a mobile hospital, made their final checks. By early afternoon, the transports were airborne and heading for Ophir on the southern tip of the Sinai peninsula; the Boeing too began the first leg of a journey that would take it to Kenya's Nairobi Airport. Operation Thunderball, the plan to rescue 105 Jewish hostages held by terrorists at Entebbe, Uganda's international airport, was under way.

The crisis faced by the Israelis began at 1210 hours on 27 June, when four terrorists, two members of the German Baader-Meinhof gang and two members of the Popular Front for the Liberation of Palestine, hijacked Air France Flight 139, with 12 crew and 246 passengers on board, as it flew from Tel Aviv to Paris via Athens. After the takeover, the passenger jet was diverted to Benghazi in Libya, where it was refuelled, and then flew south, landing at Entebbe at 0315 on the 28th. Uganda's ruler, Field-Marshal Idi Amin Dada, was no friend of the Israelis and welcomed the terrorists, who used the airport's old terminal to hold the hostages. On 29 June, the hijackers, organised and supported by a highly developed international terror network,

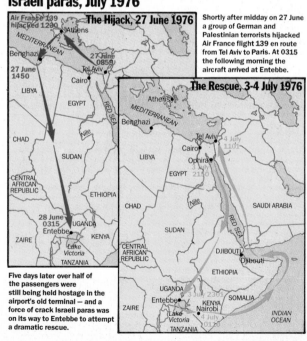

Entebbe
Israeli paras, July 1976

Shortly after midday on 27 June a group of German and Palestinian terrorists hijacked Air France flight 139 en route from Tel Aviv to Paris. At 0315 the following morning the aircraft arrived at Entebbe.

Five days later over half of the passengers were still being held hostage in the airport's old terminal – and a force of crack Israeli paras was on its way to Entebbe to attempt a dramatic rescue.

demanded the release of 53 of their comrades held in Israel, France, West Germany, Kenya and Switzerland.

Initially, the Israeli government was unwilling to risk the lives of the non-Jewish hostages in a rescue attempt, but when the other passengers were released, senior politicians and military leaders, including Chief-of-Staff Lieutenant-General Mordechai Gur, Prime Minister Yitzhak Rabin and Minister of Defence Shimon Peres, accepted a daring plan proposed by Major-General Dan Shomron, the director of infantry and paratroops. After days of intensive preparation, the assault teams left Ophir airbase on 3 July; ahead lay a 4800km journey to Entebbe.

Fifteen minutes after the last aircraft left Ophir, a second Boeing was on its way south from an airbase in central Israel. It would also land at Ophir then follow the transports – three hours behind to allow for its higher speed. On board were Major-General Kuti Adam, another senior officer, and a team of communications officers. Their job was to circle Entebbe, providing a vital radio link between the men on the ground, the planners in Israel and the medics who had been flown to Nairobi Airport.

In the bellies of the aircraft, the soldiers sprawled alongside their vehicles

In the cockpits of the four transport planes which were now flying low over the Gulf of Suez, below the reach of hostile radar surveillance, the pilots were studying a batch of aerial photographers of Entebbe Airport taken from Kenyan airspace over Lake Victoria. In the bellies of the aircraft, the soldiers of the assault teams, and the doctors and medics who were to land with them, sprawled alongside their vehicles catching whatever sleep they could.

Turning westward, the four Hercules headed into the African continent over Ethiopia. The weather was stormy, forcing the pilots to divert northwards close to the Sudanese frontier. However, there were no fears of detection; it was unlikely that any alert radar operator would be able to identify the planes as Israeli and the storm would wreak havoc with any incoming signals on their screens. Later, on the approach to Lake Victoria, the aircraft hit storm clouds towering in a solid mass from ground level to 13,000m. There was no time to go round, and no way to go above – they just ploughed through.

Lieutenant-Colonel 'S' held the lead plane straight on course; his cargo of 86 officers and men and the forward command post of Major-General Dan Shomron with all their vehicles and equipment had to be on the ground according to a precise timetable.

Lieutenant-Colonel 'S' kept the aircraft on a southerly course, then banked sharply to line up on Entebbe's main runway from the southwest. In the distance he could see that the runway lights were on. Behind him, in the cargo compartment, Lieutenant-Colonel Jonathan 'Yoni' Netanyahu's men,

Above: The Mercedes disguised as Idi Amin's personal car that was part of the Israeli deception plan to fool the guards at Entebbe airport.

the first assault wave, were piling into a black Mercedes, disguised to resemble Amin's personal car, and two Land-Rovers. The car engines were already running, and members of the aircrew were standing by to release the restraining cables.

At 2301 hours, only 30 seconds behind the pre-planned schedule, Lieutenant-Colonel 'S' brought the aircraft in to touch down at Entebbe in the wake of a scheduled cargo flight that unwittingly covered the landing. The rear ramp of the Hercules was already open, and the vehicles were on the ground and moving away before the plane rolled to a stop. A handful of paratroops had already jumped out of the aircraft to place emergency beacons next to the runway lights, in case the control tower shut them down.

The Mercedes and its escorts moved down the connecting road to the airport's old terminal building as fast as they could, consistent with the appearance of a senior officer's entourage. On the approaches to the tarmac apron in front of the building, two Ugandan sentries faced the oncoming vehicles, aimed their carbines, and shouted an order to stop. There was no choice, and no time to argue. The first shots from the Mercedes were from silenced pistols. One Ugandan fell and the other ran in the direction of the old control tower. The Ugandan on the ground was groping for his carbine. A para responded with a burst of fire. Muki, Netanyahu's second-in-command, and his team jumped from the car and ran the last 40m to the walkway in front of the building. The first entrance was blocked; the paras raced to a second.

After a searching debate with Netanyahu, Muki had decided to break a cardinal rule of the IDF. Junior officers usually lead the first wave of an assault, but Muki felt it important to be up front, in case there was need to make quick decisions about changes in plan. Tearing along the walkway, he was fired on by a Ugandan. Muki responded, killing him. A terrorist stepped out of the main door of the old terminal to see what the fuss was, and rapidly returned the way he had come.

Muki then discovered that the magazine of his carbine was empty. The normal procedure would have been to step aside and let someone else take the lead. He decided against this, and groped to change magazines on the run. The young officer behind him, realising what was happening, came up alongside. The two of them, and one other soldier, reached the door together – Amnon, the young lieutenant, on the left, Muki in the centre, and the trooper to the right.

A hijacker managed to loose off a burst of fire, but his bullets were high

The terrorist who had ventured out was now standing to the left of the door. Amnon fired, followed by Muki. Across the room, a terrorist rose to his feet and fired at the hostages sprawled around him, most of whom had been trying to get some sleep. Muki took care of him with two shots. Over to the right, another member of the hijacker's team managed to loose off a burst at the intruders, but his bullets were high, hitting a window and showering glass into the room. The trooper aimed and fired.

In the background, a loudhailer was booming in Hebrew and English, 'This is the IDF. Stay down.' From a nearby mattress, a young man launched himself at the trio in the doorway and was cut down by a carbine burst. The man was a bewildered hostage. Muki's troopers fanned out through the room and into the corridor to the washroom beyond – but all resistance was over.

The second assault team had meanwhile raced through another doorway into a hall where the off-duty terrorists spent their spare time. Two men in civilian clothes walked calmly towards them. Assuming that they were hostages, the soldiers held their fire. Suddenly, one of the men raised his hand and threw a grenade. The troopers dropped to the ground. A machine-gun burst eliminated their adversaries and the grenade exploded harmlessly.

Netanyahu's third team from the Land-Rovers moved to silence any opposition from the Ugandan soldiers stationed near the windows on the floor above. On the way up the stairs, they met two soldiers. The troopers killed them.

While his men circulated through the hall, calming the shocked hostages and tending the wounded, Muki was called out to the tarmac. There he found a doctor kneeling

The officer in charge of medical support, Doctor Jossi Faktor (above), describes his part in the Entebbe operation: 'In addition to our usual medical supplies, we carried lots of "space blankets" (aluminium sheets used for burn wounds) and large, old-fashioned milk pails. Both were useful: the sheets were used to cover the hostages and Air France crew, who had insufficient clothing, and the pails were used as giant sick bags.

'Being the last Hercules to land at Entebbe and the first to leave, we spent less than one hour on the ground. We spent the short flight to Nairobi evaluating and stabilising the condition of the wounded soldiers and hostages. However, our desperate attempts to resuscitate "Yoni" were to no avail.

'The hostages were shocked and excited; the soldiers emotionally exhausted. Yet only a few managed to doze off after 36 hours without sleep.'

4X-FE

Above: Israeli paras in training, disembarking vehicles from a Hercules transport. Heavily armed jeeps played a crucial role in the plan, for they enabled the Israelis to maintain control of the critical area of the airport for the period necessary to get the hostages out of the old terminal building and into the aircraft.

over his commanding officer. Netanyahu had remained outside the building to supervise all three assault teams. A bullet from the top of the old control tower had hit him in the back. While the troopers silenced the fire from above, he was dragged into the shelter of an overhanging wall by the walkway.

The assault on the old terminal was completed within three minutes after the lead plane had landed. Now, in rapid succession, its three companions came in to touch down at Entebbe. By 2308 hours, all of Thunderball Force was on the ground. The runway lights shut down as the third plane came in to land, but it didn't matter – the beacons did the job well enough.

With clockwork precision, armoured personnel carriers roared off the ramp of the second transport to take up position to the front and rear of the old terminal, while infantrymen from the first and third planes ran to secure all access roads to the airport and to take over the new terminal and control tower. The tower was vital for the safe evacuation of the hostages and their rescuers. In a brief clash at the new terminal, Sergeant Hershko Surin fell wounded. The fourth plane taxied to a holding position near the old terminal,

As soon as Air France Flight 139 was hijacked, Israeli troops began preparing for military action. As the crisis developed, the target and the method of attack became clearer, and Netanyahu's paras began intensive training at a remote airbase, using a mock-up of the old terminal at Entebbe. It was during this period, when the speediest means of reaching the terminal after the initial landing were being considered that the suggestion was made to use a Mercedes like that of Idi Amin in order to confuse the Ugandan airport guards.

While the assault troops were putting their plans together, the Israeli Air Force was also engaged in intensive practice, to accustom its crack pilots to the precise conditions they would encounter – landing a Hercules at night on an unknown airstrip, perhaps in the face of hostile fire, was a daunting prospect, that needed the highest skills and the coolest heads.

Although they had less than a week to prepare, the pilots and men who had to carry out the rescue were quite ready when they heard the order to go on 3 July. Their waiting was now over, and they could put their abilities to the test.

ready to take on the hostages. The engines were left running. A team of air force technicians were already hard at work off-loading heavy fuel pumps to transfer Idi Amin's precious aviation fuel into the thirsty tanks of the lead transport – a process that would take well over an hour.

Meanwhile, as planned, the medical corps' Boeing had landed at Nairobi, at 2205 hours. General Benny Peled, the GOC air force, was able to radio Lieutenant-Colonel 'S' that it was possible to refuel in Kenya's capital. Unable to raise Shomron on the operational radio, and uncomfortable with the situation on the ground – the Ugandans were firing tracer at random, while the aircraft with engines running were vulnerable at the fuel tanks – Peled decided to make use of the Nairobi option.

Muki radioed Shomron to report that the building and surroundings were secure, and to inform him that Netanyahu had been hit. Although they were ahead of schedule, there was no point in waiting around (possibly allowing the Ugandans the time to bring up reinforcements). The fourth Hercules was ordered to move closer to the old terminal. Muki's men and the other soldiers around the building formed two lines from the doorway to the ramp of the plane;

Above: Rigorous training provided the cohesion and automatic battle skills that the Israelis demonstrated at Entebbe.
Far right: Idi Amin, ruler of Uganda.

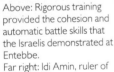

Hercules No. 1
2301 The lead plane touches down. Men detailed to secure the runway disembark, followed by the assault group.

Hercules No. 2
After an interval of several minutes, the second aircraft arrives and further troops deploy.

Hercules No. 3
The aircraft bearing reserve forces touches down as the main runway lighting is extinguished.

Hercules No. 4
2308 The final Hercules is on the ground. Further reserve forces disembark and the aircraft taxies towards the old terminal to pick up rescued hostages.

Route of
Hercules Nos. 1 – 3

Route of
Hercules No. 4

Command Group and Tac HQ move out from the first aircraft and assume command.

Group D deploys in APCs to the old terminal.

Group A drives down the taxiway and assaults the old terminal.

Group C, the reserve force, moves down to the old terminal on foot to assist with the evacuation.

Group B secures the main runway and takes the new terminal and control tower.

Key
Operation Thunderball

Operation Thunderball: routes of Hercules transports

Operation Thunderball: routes of assault groups

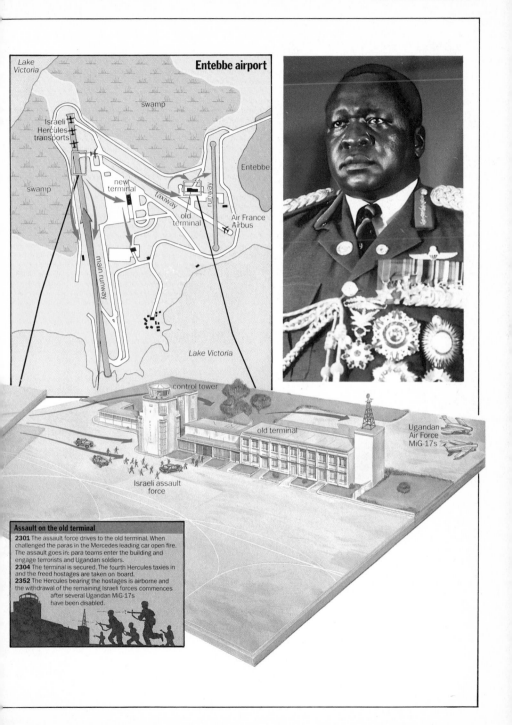

Entebbe airport

Lake Victoria

swamp

Israeli Hercules transports

swamp

new terminal

taxiway

old terminal

Entebbe

Air France Airbus

main runway

Lake Victoria

control tower

old terminal

Ugandan Air Force MiG-17s

Israeli assault force

Assault on the old terminal

2301 The assault force drives to the old terminal. When challenged the paras in the Mercedes leading car open fire. The assault goes in: para teams enter the building and engage terrorists and Ugandan soldiers.

2304 The terminal is secured. The fourth Hercules taxies in and the freed hostages are taken on board.

2352 The Hercules bearing the hostages is airborne and the withdrawal of the remaining Israeli forces commences after several Ugandan MiG-17s have been disabled.

79

Above: After their triumphant return on 4 July, the assault teams and their commander (Major-General Dan Shomron, standing third from left) were congratulated by Defence Minister Shimon Peres (far left).
Below: A returning Hercules taxies to a halt.

Left: Scenes of unrestrained jubilation greeted the arrival of the freed hostages at Lod airport on the morning of 4 July. Watched by thousands, they walked off the plane – their ordeal at an end.

no chances would be taken that a bewildered hostage could wander off into the night or blunder into the aircraft's propellers.

As the hostages straggled out, the heads of each family were stopped at the ramp and asked to check that all their kin were present. Captain Bacos, the pilot of Flight 139, was quietly requested to perform the same task for his family – the crew of the airliner. Behind them, the old terminal was empty but for the bodies of six terrorists, among them Gabriele Kröcher-Tiedemann and a blond-haired man, Wilfried Böse, both members of the Baader-Meinhof gang. Seven other terrorists, who were at Entebbe to meet the

Above: Lieutenant-Colonel Jonathan Netanyahu, the only member of the raiding party killed during Operation Thunderball.

hostages when they first arrived, were also killed.

It took seven minutes to load the precious cargo of humanity, while a pick-up truck, brought specially for the purpose, ferried out the dead and wounded, including Netanyahu. The paratroops made a last check of the main building, then signalled the aircrew to close up and go. At 2352 hours the craft was airborne and on its way to Nairobi. Inside, doctors tended seven wounded hostages. Two had died during the rescue and a third, Mrs Dora Bloch, moved to a hospital in Uganda's capital, Kampala, before the raid, was later murdered.

An infantry team fired machine-gun bursts into Ugandan MiGs

At the other end of the airfield, an infantry team fired machine-gun bursts into seven Ugandan Air Force MiGs. There was no point in letting Ugandan pilots attempt pursuit. The paras reloaded their vehicles and equipment. Their job done, they were airborne at 0012 hours on the 4th. Behind them, their comrades completed their tasks. At 0040, the last members of the assault force left Entebbe.

Thirty minutes after the final departure, the communications Boeing and the first Hercules touched down at Nairobi and taxied to the fuel tanks in a quiet corner of the airport. Sergeant Surin, who was seriously wounded, was transferred to the hospital Boeing. Two hostages whose wounds needed immediate care in a fully equipped hospital were loaded into a waiting station wagon and taken into Nairobi. At 0204 the remaining passengers and crew of Flight 139 were airborne on the last leg of their long journey home. In Lieutenant-Colonel S's aircraft, the paratroops were sunk in their own private thoughts. Despite all the efforts of the doctors, Netanyahu was dead. The mission was later renamed Operation Jonathan in his memory.

Early in the morning, the lead Hercules flew low over Eilat, at the southern tip of Israel. The tired airmen in the cockpit were astonished to see people in the streets below waving and clapping. The plane flew on to land at an air force base in central Israel. Here, the hostages were fed and given a chance to shake off the trauma. The wounded were taken off to hospital, and psychologists circulated among the rest.

It was mid-morning when a Hercules transport of the Israeli Air Force touched down at Lod airport outside Tel Aviv, rolled to a stop and opened its rear ramp to release its cargo of men, women and children into the outstretched arms of their relatives and friends, watched by a crowd of thousands. The ordeal was over. By the rescue of the hostages the Israelis had shown the rest of the world that terrorism could be met and defeated by the clinical application of controlled force. In the supreme test of their professional skills, the Israeli paras had pulled off an amazing coup, the reverberations of which spread worldwide.

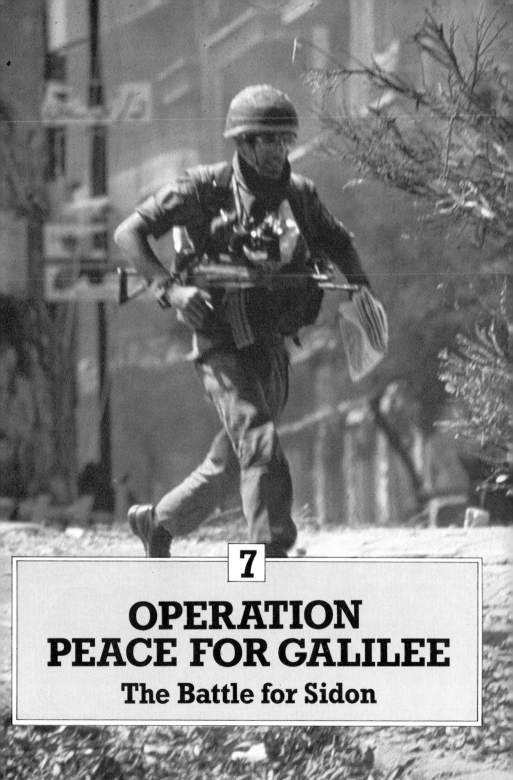

7

OPERATION PEACE FOR GALILEE
The Battle for Sidon

The IDF invasion of southern
Lebanon, which began on 6 June
1982, was ostensibly carried out,
in the words of Israeli prime
minister Menachem Begin, to 'put
all settlements in Galilee out of
reach of terrorist artillery'.
Controlling a 40km belt of
territory to the north of Israel's
northern border would have been
enough to achieve this goal, but
some Israeli politicians were also
intent on destroying the PLO's
military infrastructure in Lebanon,
and establishing a pro-Israeli
government in Beirut. Moving
north on three main axes in a
classic example of blitzkrieg
warfare, IDF units succeeded
either in capturing or outflanking
all the PLO's strongpoints. After
major battles at Tyre, Sidon, and
Beaufort Castle, by 11 June the
IDF were laying siege to Beirut
itself, with 14,000 PLO soldiers
trapped in the city.

ON 9 JUNE 1982, a force of Israeli paratroops was faced with the
dangerous task of clearing the town of Sidon of PLO guerrillas entrenched there. Supported by tanks and artillery
putting down a barrage 400m ahead of them, the paras
advanced along the main road. The tanks fired at PLO
positions in small buildings and in the bottom stories of the
high-rise blocks, while artillery fire and air strikes were
directed on the buildings where resistance was toughest. In
spite of this heavy and well-coordinated support, however,
the paras had once more to show their mettle as elite infantry
– fighting at close quarters to mop up in the town.

This was strange, dangerous, exhausting work – the paras
would climb up 20 flights of stairs in a tall residential block,
expecting to be fired upon at any moment, with death lurking
round every corner. Often the sights that greeted them were
surreal. As one soldier described it later: 'We burst into one
apartment. There was a large living room filled with heavy,
antique furniture and glass-doored cupboards. Thick car-
pets were on the floor. In the middle of the room stood a
105mm anti-tank gun. The rear wall was black from the
constant firing.'

This was not the sort of battle for flashy gestures, for vain
self-sacrifice. The para commander, Colonel 'Y', preferred a

slow, methodical advance, to keep casualties to a minimum. The same tactic was used over and over again: suppress sniper fire with tank and artillery shells and air strikes, enter the building, mop up, exit, rest and regroup – then do it all over again. In this painstaking way the paras cleared the main road into Sidon and adjoining streets, but the job was still only half-done. Large numbers of PLO men remained in the ancient Casbah area of the town and in the Ein El Hilwe refugee camp – the centre of PLO military activity.

Operation Peace for Galilee, the Israeli invasion of southern Lebanon, had begun on 6 June 1982 with a combined land and sea assault. The paras were put ashore before dawn on the next day 3km to the north of Sidon in the largest ever amphibious landings undertaken by the IDF. The first group to land, paras supported by naval commandos, prepared the landing area for the main force and set up a formal command post. They also laid ambushes and mined roads, but the PLO response to the landing was muted – just a few 'Katyusha' rockets fired out to sea. The main landing force consisted of paratroops in M113 Armoured Personnel Carriers (APCs), supported by naval, tank and artillery fire.

Sidon was an important strategic position, lying on Lebanon's main coastal communication route. It was also an Al

Page 83: An Israeli paratrooper runs for cover during the streetfighting in Sidon.
Below: Israeli armoured personnel carriers and tanks make an amphibious landing on the coast of Lebanon to outflank Palestinian positions. Israeli paratroopers provided the spearhead of the landings to the north of Sidon.

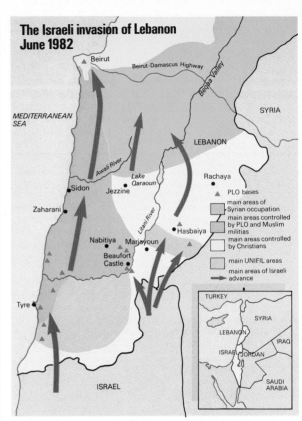

The Israeli invasion of Lebanon June 1982

MEDITERRANEAN SEA

Beirut

Beirut-Damascus Highway

Bekaa Valley

SYRIA

LEBANON

Awali River

Lake Qaraoun

Rachaya

Sidon

Jezzine

Zaharani

Litani River

Hasbaiya

Nabitiya

Marjayoun

Beaufort Castle

Tyre

ISRAEL

▲ PLO bases

main areas of Syrian occupation

main areas controlled by PLO and Muslim militias

main areas controlled by Christians

main UNIFIL areas

→ main areas of Israeli advance

TURKEY

SYRIA

LEBANON

IRAQ

ISRAEL JORDAN

SAUDI ARABIA

Below: Israeli paratroopers in a 'Zelda' (a US-supplied M113 modified by the IDF) on the road to Sidon.

Fatah naval base (Fatah was one of the most important groups within the PLO) and an arms supply centre from which thousands of weapons were transferred to Arab guerrillas throughout Lebanon. Tanks, missiles, smallarms and ammunition from the Soviet bloc countries, Syria, Libya, North Korea and even the United States passed through the town. The PLO military infrastructure – military posts, HQs, stores, gun platforms and observation posts – was sited in the midst of the civilian population. Defences were based on a closely built network of high-rise buildings and concealed bunkers, prepared for an Israeli attack from the south. The defenders were some 1500 Al Fatah guerrillas from the El Kastel Brigade, reinforced by units retreating from the IDF invasion of the south that had begun the previous day. The El Kastel Brigade had also built fortifications in the mountains overlooking the coastal strip and was supported by the Palestinians in the nearby Ein El Hilwe refugee camp.

The paras moved in from the north in a smooth, professional operation

Operation Peace for Galilee was planned as a swift, deep advance, bypassing pockets of resistance, which were to be dealt with later. However, the PLO's secure entrenchment in the heart of Sidon, and the town's strategic position on the coast, made it impossible to bypass. Sidon was duly surrounded on the morning of 7 June and the paras moved in from the north in a smooth, professional operation.

At noon on the 7th, units of the Golani Brigade with armoured support began an advance on Ein El Hilwe in the southeastern suburbs. Another combined force of Golani infantry and armour moved onto the ridges overlooking the town from the east. The paratroops were now ordered to open the main north–south road through Sidon to Israeli traffic on its way north towards Beirut, and then to join up with the southern force for an attack on Ein El Hilwe. This mission was initially to have been given to one of the forces moving north, but because of the fierce resistance that the IDF was encountering in Sidon, it was decided to send in the paras.

The next morning, 8 June, the Voice of Israel radio station broadcast the following message on its Arabic network:

'To the residents of Sidon: Announcement number 10. IDF forces are about to complete removing the remnants of trapped Palestinian terrorist nests in your city. The IDF is doing its utmost in order to avoid injuring the civilian population in the city, but will uproot anyone holding arms. The fate of the trapped terrorists has already been sealed, after their commanders abandoned them. Residents of Sidon, your brother residents of Tyre hearkened to IDF calls and evacuated their town in order to enable the elimination of terrorist nests in that city. Residents of Tyre have been returning to their homes since last night and are better protected and more secure than at any time. Residents of Sidon, the IDF will do its utmost to avoid injuring you – the unarmed citizens of the city. For your

CIVILIAN CASUALTIES

One of the problems for the IDF in their invasion of Lebanon was that the PLO had built its defences in the midst of the civilian population. In Sidon, for example, the Church of Mar Elias housed Al Fatah soldiers and five tanks, and in the refugee camp of Ein El Hilwe the government hospital was turned into an artillery emplacement. During the fighting, snipers fired from the hospital windows with patients still in the beds behind them. Inevitably, as the IDF entered Sidon many civilians were caught up in the fighting, and large amounts of property and housing were destroyed. The official Israeli figure for civilian dead in Nabatieh, Tyre and Sidon is 316 – IDF casualties for the whole campaign were 100 dead and 600 wounded.

own good, quickly distance yourself from the area of danger. The IDF will enable you to return safely to your homes as soon as possible. You have been warned. Remember, your lives are in your own hands. The Israeli Defence Forces.'

This warning followed several others that called on civilians to: 'Deny armed elements the use of your houses and neighbourhoods as combat positions,' 'Stay in your homes and do not go out,' 'Suspend from your windows or balconies a white sheet which is clearly visible from the street,' and 'Constantly listen to announcements that will be broadcast on the Voice of Israel.' At the same time, Israeli Air Force (IAF) aircraft dropped leaflets on the town calling on the civilian population not to be drawn into the fighting, but to leave their homes and gather on the beach within two hours. When this period had passed, the IDF commanders felt that armour, artillery and air strikes could be used against the PLO in the town.

Far left: An Israeli Zelda moves through the streets of Sidon, while the town's inhabitants display white flags to prevent the Israelis from confusing them with Palestinian soldiers.
Left: The city of Sidon with the Palestinian camp of Ein El Hilwe in the foreground.
Above: Two Israeli 155mm howitzers shell Palestinian positions.

Above: A paratrooper platoon HQ group gives fire support during the fighting in Sidon. To counter Palestinian snipers, the paratroopers relied on fire support from their own heavy weapons or tanks.

At noon, the paratroopers began their advance, reinforced by more tanks and artillery that had been landed from the sea. In order to save time, it was decided to ignore any building not known as a terrorist emplacement or from which there was no firing. The paras, again commanded by Colonel 'Y', advanced down the main street in two lines, close to the buildings on both sides. Tanks and more lightly armoured self-propelled 155mm artillery pieces followed. The self-propelled guns were a necessity, due to the limited elevation of the tank guns. Resistance was slight at first – just sporadic bursts of sniper fire. This was silenced by point-blank fire from the artillery into the buildings occupied by snipers. But the deeper the paras advanced into the town, the heavier the sniper fire became. Tank and artillery commanders were prime targets for the PLO defenders, and the advance became achingly slow and dangerous. Two Syrian MiGs made a bombing run over the Israeli column, causing no casualties but adding to the tension. By evening, the para commanders knew that they would not accomplish their mission that day. The southern force attacking Ein El Hilwe reached the same conclusion and also withdrew.

Right: A group of paratroopers moves cautiously along a street. As the Israelis moved deeper into Sidon, they encountered heavy sniper fire. It took a coordinated artillery barrage in support of the paratroopers to clear part of the town.

Above: An Israeli soldier watches the movement of Palestinian troops near his position. The Palestinian forces in the Lebanon had built up enormous stocks of arms in weapons caches throughout the country. T34 and T55 tanks, armoured personnel carriers and a total of 30,000 assault rifles were found in 540 caches.

The following morning, 9 June, it was decided to give all possible support to the paras. Clearing the main road was now a priority, to maintain a flow of supplies to the armoured units pushing ever northwards. The attack on Ein El Hilwe was delayed and all the artillery in the area was placed at the paras' disposal. This was crucial, for behind a coordinated barrage from tanks, artillery and aircraft, the paras, moving steadily from building to building, finally succeeded in winkling out the PLO defenders.

With the main street clear, however, the Casbah remained a problem – the narrow twisting alleyways of this old city providing an ideal site for the remaining PLO men to make a last stand. This was a situation that had been foreseen by the IDF commanders, for at their pre-invasion briefing the chief of IDF military intelligence, Major-General Yehoshua Sagie, had specifically warned of the folly of streetfighting in the Casbah: 'In 1976, the Syrians attempted to enter Sidon, against the wishes of the PLO. The Syrians were tied down for seven days on the outskirts and could not break a way in. In that battle they lost many tanks, APCs and men. Many were taken prisoner.' This advice was echoed by an anti-PLO Sidon 'Mukhtar' (elder): 'Destroy it,' he said. 'Do not break yourselves and throw away all you have gained so far by trying to enter the place.'

After calling on the PLO guerrillas to surrender, Israeli

artillery fired a number of warning rounds into the Casbah. There was no response to the call for a surrender, and so a massive artillery barrage followed, reducing parts of the old city to rubble and forcing the few surviving defenders to capitulate. Thankful that the Casbah no longer posed a threat, the indefatigable paras headed off to join up with the Golani units for the attack on Ein El Hilwe – another successful operation for the IDF.

The battle for Sidon had been a gruelling test of military skill and courage. The high professional standards of the Israeli paratroopers had once again, as on so many occasions since the mid-1950s, allowed them to defeat a determined and well-entrenched enemy. The Israeli paras had done it again.

Above: An Israeli paratrooper in the Lebanon, armed with an M16. During their campaign in the Lebanon, the paras once again displayed the fighting qualities that have made them one of the world's elite military forces.

CHRONOLOGY

1948 The Israeli Parachute Corps is established. Yoel Palgi is appointed its first commander.

1949 Yehuda Harari replaces Palgi as paratroop commander; he reorganises the unit to improve training and discipline.

1953 Unit 101, a special commando force for reprisal raids, was formed.

1954 Unit 101 and the paratroopers are integrated. Together they attack an Egyptian position at Kissufim.

1955 Paratroopers attack an Egyptian camp in the Gaza Strip. During the next year the paratroopers conduct many retaliatory raids on Arab positions near the Israeli borders.

1956 The Parachute Corps makes its first combat jump at the Mitla Pass during the Sinai campaign against Egypt in October and November.

1965 The newly-formed Palestinian Liberation Organisation (PLO) launches a series of attacks against Israel. The paratroopers are sent on raids of PLO bases to halt these incursions.

1966 The paratroopers carry out further reprisal raids against PLO bases.

1967 Israel and its Arab neighbours fight the Six-Day War in June. Units of the Israeli Parachute Corps are involved in the capture of Jerusalem, the seizure of the Gaza Strip, the advance to the Suez Canal and battles in the Golan Heights.

1968 War of Attrition begins between Egypt, the PLO and Israel. During the next two years both sides conduct raids, artillery bombardments and aerial attacks on each other. The Israeli Parachute Corps plays a prominent part in Israeli operations.

1970 A US-arranged cease-fire brings the War of Attrition to an end.

1973 In February and April the Parachute Corps launches raids against PLO targets in Lebanon. During the Yom Kippur War in October paratroopers are involved in battles on the Golan Heights and the Suez Canal.

1982 Paratroopers play a leading role in the Israeli attack on PLO and Syrian positions in Lebanon, Operation Peace for Galilee.

FURTHER READING

Adan, Avraham (Bren) *On the Banks of the Suez*, Arms and Armour Press, London 1980
Eshel, David (ed.) *Elite Fighting Units*, Arco Publishing, New York 1984
Herzog, Chaim *The Arab-Israeli Wars*, Arms and Armour Press, London 1982
Hogg, Ian *Israeli War Machine*, Quarto Publishing 1983
Pimlott, John (ed.) *The Middle East Conflicts*, Orbis Publishing 1983
Rothenburg, Gunther *The Anatomy of the Israeli Army*, Arms and Armour Press, London 1979

INDEX

Page numbers in *italics* refer to illustrations. The following abbreviations are used:
Bde = Brigade, Btn = Battalion, Div = Division